ANTHROPOLOGICAL PAPERS

MUSEUM OF ANTHROPOLOGY, UNIVERSITY OF MICHIGAN
NO. 25

STUDIES IN THE NATURAL RADIOACTIVITY OF PREHISTORIC MATERIALS

EDITORS   ARTHUR J. JELINEK
                       JAMES E. FITTING

CONTRIBUTORS   JAMES E. FITTING
                       CHARLES E. CLELAND
                       LEWIS R. BINFORD
                       ARTHUR J. JELINEK

ANN ARBOR
THE UNIVERSITY OF MICHIGAN, 1965

© 1965 by the Regents of the University of Michigan
The Museum of Anthropology
All rights reserved

ISBN (print): 978-1-949098-20-4
ISBN (ebook): 978-1-951519-43-8

Browse all of our books at
sites.lsa.umich.edu/archaeology-books.

Order our books from the University of Michigan
Press at www.press.umich.edu.

For permissions, questions, or manuscript queries,
contact Museum publications by email at umma-pubs@umich.edu or visit the Museum website at
lsa.umich.edu/ummaa.

PREFACE

The following reports are the result of work carried out intermittently since 1956 to explore the possible usefulness of gross natural radioactivity of archeological and paleontological specimens in studies of chronology and material origin. This research has been conducted under the sponsorship of the Michigan Memorial—Phoenix Project (MMPP 132). Professor Frederick P. Thieme directed the project from its inception in the fall of 1956 until 1958, when Professor James B. Griffin assumed the direction. Since the fall of 1961 the project has been under my direction. Research assistants on the project include Lewis R. Binford (1958-1960), James E. Fitting (1961-1963), Charles E. Cleland (summer, 1962) and myself (1957-1958).

All of the research was carried out by persons whose primary field of interest was prehistoric archaeology and our chief interest in the investigations was the application of these techniques to archaeological problems.

We should like to take this opportunity to express our gratitude to the following: in some of the more technical difficulties we were fortunate in being able to seek the sympathetic advice of Professor H. R. Crane of the Department of Physics, University of Michigan. During the summer of 1963 Dr. Iqbal Qureshi of the Pakistan AEC generously helped Fitting in an analysis of several specimens on a multichannel analyzer. Miss Patricia Dahlstrom has aided the project by recording sample counts and backgrounds over the past several years. However, our technical advisers should not be held responsible for the interpretations presented in this volume.

In presenting this study the reports have been separated into two major categories: those primarily concerned with method; and those dealing with specific problems of chronology. The author and date of completion of each report is given with the report. The authors were given opportunities to revise their own manuscripts in the spring of 1964.

Arthur J. Jelinek

CONTENTS

Introduction. *James E. Fitting* 1

PART I

Methodology. *James E. Fitting* 4

Effect of Sample Preparation on Measurements of Natural Radioactivity. *James E. Fitting* 8

The Effect of Particle Size on the Beta Activity of Three Samples of Mixed Composition from Research Cave, Calloway County, Missouri. *Charles E. Cleland and Arthur J. Jelinek* 14

The Effect of Differential Charring on the Beta Activity of Bone from the Pecos River Valley, New Mexico. *Charles E. Cleland* 18

Heat Alteration and Radioactivity in Fossil Bone. *James E. Fitting* 20

Internal Variation in Radioactivity of a Standard Sample. *James E. Fitting* 23

PART II

Radioactive Assay of Bone Material from the Riverside Cemetery, Menominee County, Michigan. *Lewis R. Binford* 28

Radiometric Analysis of Bone and Soil Material from Lloyd's Rock Hole, Bedford County, Pennsylvania. *Lewis R. Binford* ... 32

Analysis of Bone Material from the Medicine Crow Site (39 BF 2) Buffalo County, South Dakota. *Lewis R. Binford* 41

Report on the Radiometric Analysis of Animal and Fish Bones from the Feeheley Site (20 SA 128) Saginaw County, Michigan. *James E. Fitting* 45

The Beta Activity of Human Bone from the Feeheley and Andrews Sites, Saginaw County, Michigan. *Charles E. Cleland* .. 53

Beta Activity of Animal Burials at the Juntunen Site (20 MK 1) on Bois Blanc Island. *Charles E. Cleland* 56

Report on the Beta Activity of Five Bone Samples from the Palegawra Site in Iraq. *Charles E. Cleland* 59

The Beta Activity of Four Bone Samples from Cueva Reclau, Gerona Province, Spain. *Charles E. Cleland* 62

A Study of Natural Radioactivity in Osteological Materials from the Blackwater Draw Number 1 Locality, Roosevelt County, New Mexico. *James E. Fitting* 64

A Gamma Ray Analysis of Fossil Bone from Blackwater Draw
    Number 1 Locality. *James E. Fitting* 77
Addendum: Chemical Isolation of Radioactive Elements in
    Archaeological and Paleontological Material. *James E. Fitting*.. 89
Summary. *Arthur J. Jelinek* 93
References 95

INTRODUCTION

James E. Fitting

The study of natural radioactivity in prehistoric materials is not a recent innovation. As Davidson and Atkin (1953) pointed out, the British physicist Strutt reported on the natural radioactivity of fossil bone in 1908. Studies made by Herbert (1947) and Hill (1950) indicated that fossil bone had a higher level of radioactivity than had modern bone. Jaffee and Sherwood (1951) demonstrated that there was, in general, a higher uranium content in the ribs of fossil manatee from Florida than in the ribs of modern manatee. They also noted the great variation in uranium content of fossil material.

One of the first attempts to use natural radioactivity for the solution of a paleontological problem was the work of Bowie and Davidson (1955) on the Piltdown fossils. Oakley (1950) using relative amounts of flourine in fossils reportedly recovered from the Piltdown gravels, had demonstrated that much of this material was not of Lower or Middle Pleistocene derivation. The radiometric examination of Bowie and Davidson confirmed and elaborated this position.

Oakley (1955) included radiometric analysis in his discussion of techniques for relative dating of bone.

A radiometric examination of fossil bone from the Scharbauer site in Texas was published in 1958 by Oakley and Rixon. As a part of a chemical analysis of the bone the radioactivity of human skull fragments was the crucial factor in determining their stratigraphic origin. They reported an increase in radioactivity over a period of time. Specimens from the lower levels of the deposits showed a higher level of radioactivity than those from the upper levels. Oakley and Rixon examined the potentialities of this method of analysis for developing an absolute chronology but concluded on the basis of their work that this was not possible.

By 1958 the Michigan Memorial—Phoenix Project Number 132 was in operation, carrying out a series of studies of the variables affecting the use of natural radioactivity in problems of relative chronology. A large backlog of manuscript reports has accumulated over the past seven years, and frequently research has made papers obsolete before the first drafts of research reports could be edited, standardized, and prepared for publication. A portion of the project research has already been published by Jelinek (1960*a*: 933, 1960*b*: 179) Binford (1960, 1962) and Jelinek and Fitting (1963). The present volume is a selection of the more significant unpublished reports of the past several years. The date of preparation is given for each report to indicate the relationship to later work.

The several papers covering aspects of the Michigan Memorial—Phoenix Project Number 132 which have already been published are briefly summarized below.

Jelinek (1960*a*, p. 933) used a comparison of Alpha activity to demonstrate that material from the Foley gravel pit came from the sand and not the silt deposits in the area.

In an analysis of sherd materials Jelinek (1960*b*, p. 179) was unable to determine levels of activity sufficiently distinct to identify materials from several localities in the Pecos Valley of New Mexico. Binford (1960) prepared an extensive report on the radioactive properties of bone from the Smith site. Issued in mimeographed form, this report was distributed to approximately eighty persons concerned with the Smith site and with the significance of radioactive assay for the investigation of archaeological problems.

In 1962 Binford published an analysis of the radioactive properties of bone from the Oconto site. In this study he proposed a set of postulates which were tested by later researchers. The results of these tests are included in the first group of reports presented here.

The most recent article is a report by Jelinek and Fitting (1963) on several studies of natural radioactivity. Jelinek presented a series of Alpha and Beta measurements on material from Blackwater Draw Number 1 Locality as well as studies of other paleontological material. Jelinek's studies in this area provided the stimulus for the two papers on Blackwater Draw presented in this volume. My section of the report dealt with a series of fish, mammal, and bird bone specimens from the Late Woodland Juntunen site on Bois Blanc Island in the Straits of Mackinac. One additional paper on the Juntunen series is included in this volume.

While the above sources do not furnish a complete bibliography of papers dealing with natural radioactivity in archaeological and paleontological materials, they do suggest the pattern of development of Michigan Memorial—Phoenix Project Number 132 and the scientific base from which it originated. Additional sources, pertinent to specific problems, are cited in the individual papers mentioned.

The following volume is divided into two sections. The first deals with variables affecting the level of natural radioactivity.

The second section will be of more interest to the archaeologist since it contains a series of reports on the application of radioactive assay to specific problems in prehistory. The final paper, or Addendum is included because it suggests a line of investigation which may prove profitable for future research.

PART I

METHODOLOGY

James E. Fitting

This section concentrates on the problems of sample preparation and processing and does not deal with the mechanics of operation of our counters used by the project. It consists of procedures drawn up at the conclusion of my work on the project, based upon our experience to that time. The techniques presented here were largely developed by Cleland and myself, working under Jelinek, and are based on the previous work of Jelinek, Binford, and others.

These techniques of preparation and processing were adapted to the equipment available to the Museum of Anthropology, University of Michigan, and were developed by students of archaeology rather than by students of physics.

This information is designed to serve as a supplement to the collected project reports and is concerned with mechanical details not suitable for inclusion in the reports.

Description of Equipment

From the inception of the project until January of 1959 samples were run in a proportional radiation flow counter (Radiation Counter Laboratories Nucleometer Mark 9, Model 4). From that time until September, 1963, a flow counter incorporating anticoincidence counters, especially designed for low-level count by Professor H. R. Crane and operated by Miss Patricia Dahlstrom, was used by the project. A series of runs on the same on both counters indicate that the order equipment was less efficient in counting very low activity and more efficient in high activity samples. All such tests which we conducted indicated a predictable relationship between the results of the two counters.

Sample runs of low-level specimens on the earlier equipment were alternated with background runs in an attempt to control gross variations in background. Higher level counts (over 2X normal background) were considered against a mean background of 17.17 cpm observed over 40 one-half hour runs. The extreme ranges of variation observed in background were from 15 cpm to 20 cpm. Use of heavy shielding, the anticoincidence counter, and a device to monitor voltage fluctuation in the later equipment made some of these procedures unnecessary, although an additional calculation to correct for voltage fluctuation was used for sample runs below 10 cpm.

Designation of the Sample

Several systems of numbering samples have been used in the course of the project. Jelinek used two systems. In 1957 he used a three unit sample designation. The first number was the month of the year, the second was the date of the month and the third was the number of the sample run on that day (e.g. 6-28-3 is the third sample run through the counter on June 28, 1957). This system was abandoned in 1958 in favor of consecutive numbering of samples for a particular year. Sample 58-1 was run in June of 1958 by Jelinek.

Beginning in the fall of 1958 Binford used a numbering system based on a letter and digit combination. His sample designations were prefixed by the letter "M" followed by a digit representing a related series of specimens, a second digit representing the sample order in the series and a third digit representing the number of the run for that sample. The Smith site report, for example, contains a specimen designated M 2-50-3, which is the third run on the fiftieth sample in the Smith site series (2).

In 1961, I adopted the following system. The initial letters in the series run by Cleland and myself were PH (for Phoenix), which distinguished their runs from Binford's "M" designation (Michigan). This was followed by a digit unit which referred to the series and another digit unit which referred to the number of the specimen within the series. No additional numbers were given to additional runs since these were recorded on a single card and could be distinguished by the date of the run. Therefore, my sample run might have a sample number of PH3-55. This would be the fifty-fifth sample from the third, or Juntunen, series.

Preparation of the Sample

The specimens (with the exception of soil samples) were carefully washed to remove any foreign material and then dried thoroughly. Our tests had demonstrated that adhering soil could significantly affect the count on a specimen.

Slightly more than the required amount of the sample was weighed out preparatory to grinding the material. Most samples were pulverized with a porcelain mortar and pestle. Some more resilient samples were broken up with a hammer or heavy iron blocks before being pulverized. In some cases, such as completely fossilized bone, a file was used to remove material for a sample. The material filed from bone was so fine that it needed no further grinding.

Samples were weighed out on clean sheets of paper on a small laboratory balance.

Samples to be compared were of a uniform weight. Studies utilizing the earlier counter used 1.0 gram samples. Studies in 1961 indicated that 1.5 grams was the optimum weight for the counter designed by Crane.

We encounted special problems with soil samples. It was necessary to cover the entire surface of the sample dish with an even layer of the sample. Due to mechanical difficulties in grinding and distribution 3.0 gram samples of soil were used.

At this point, the sample number was written on the rim of the sample dish with a red grease pencil and the desired weight of the sample was poured from the paper into the sample dish. It has been mentioned that increased sample size means an increased count. The increase is not proportional, however, but follows an inverse logarithmic progression. For instance, 1.0 gram of a substance might have an activity of 100 counts per minute. A 1.5 gram preparation of the same material would have an activity of 125 counts per minute and a 2.0 gram sample would have an activity of 138 counts per minute. The count is also related to the aperture of the sample dishes. In the early phases of the project three-quarter-inch stainless steel planchets were used. Later 2.0-inch copper planchets were specially prepared for use by the project in the counter designed by Crane. There were several reasons why this size was preferable. The back-scatter and self-absorbtion, which lead to the progressively smaller increases in count with increased sample size, is minimized with the wider aperture. In addition, our sample dishes could also be run, as they were in the summer of 1963 at the School of Public Health (Environmental Health) in a beta counter which was calibrated for similar 2.0-inch planchets.

After the powder was placed in the planchet, sufficient acetone to saturate the sample was added to settle the material and furnish a more even surface. Acetone was used because of its high evaporation rate.

The planchet was gently tapped until the sample appeared uniform and compacted, after which the dish was set aside in an area free from contamination until most of the acetone evaporated (about one hour).

Because variation in moisture led to inconsistencies in the operation of the counter, once the acetone was nearly dry, the samples were placed in a dessication jar with Dryerite Crystals (anhydrous $Ca\ SO_4$) for a period of twenty-four hours.

The samples were then stored in covered boxes until run. After a sample had been run in the counter it was stored in a capped glass vial.

The sample dishes were cleaned with a toothbrush under running water and the sample number rubbed off; the dish was rinsed in dilute hydrochloric acid, followed by tap water and wiped dry. They were stored in covered containers between use.

EFFECT OF SAMPLE PREPARATION ON MEASUREMENTS OF NATURAL RADIOACTIVITY

James E. Fitting

November 1961

Series PH2 was conceived as a control project to test the effects of the size of the sample, the size of the particle within the sample and the preparation of the sample. Series PH1, a rerun of material originally run in 1958, had seemed to indicate that such factors might be significant.

Two samples of approximately 200 grams each were prepared from fragments of mammoth tusk known to have a high count. These samples were taken from the Brown Sand Wedge, Locality 1., Blackwater Draw, Roosevelt Co., N.M.) (Sellards, 1952). One sample was of washed and the other of unwashed tusk fragments. Each was powdered and then thoroughly mixed to assure uniformity.

Fifty-six runs were made with samples varying between one and three grams at .5 gram intervals. The material was graded as coarsly ground, finely ground, sifted through a number 60 screen, a number 120 screen, and a number 200 screen.

The high activity of the sample precluded the use of the cosmic ray correction factor.

From the fifty-six runs fifty samples were selected as applicable for comparison. The object of this series was to determine the difference between: (1) washed and unwashed samples; (2) weights of samples; and (3) size of particles in the samples.

Twenty-three of the washed values are higher than their unwashed counterparts. If we assume that washed and unwashed samples are part of the same population the probability of this happening would be the possible combinations of two or less divided by the number of possible combinations or two to the twenty-fifth power:

$$\frac{1 \text{ plus } 2 \text{ plus } 3 \text{ plus } \ldots \text{ plus } 24 \text{ plus } 25 \text{ plus } 1}{} = \frac{326}{49,840,128} = .000004$$

Therefore we rejected the hypotheses that the washed and unwashed samples were part of the same population and separated them for further tests.

TABLE I
Washed and Unwashed Samples
(Measured in counts per minute)

Unwashed Samples		Washed Samples		Value
Coarse	Ground	Coarse	Ground	Washed/Unwashed
1.0g	186.88	1.0g	194.76	>1
1.5g	238.54	1.5g	242.48	>1
2.0g	276.86	2.0g	270.52	<1
2.5g	301.56	2.5g	303.78	>1
3.0g	320.94	3.0g	317.92	<1
Fine	Ground	Fine	Ground	Washed/Unwashed
1.0g	192.93	1.0g	198.62	>1
1.5g	236.61	1.5g	248.34	>1
2.0g	270.94	2.0g	285.48	>1
2.5g	299.74	2.5g	306.48	>1
3.0g	320.21	3.0g	333.55	>1
Number	60 Screen	Number	60 Screen	Washed/Unwashed
1.0g	183.89	1.0g	197.92	>1
1.5g	245.98	1.5g	248.00	>1
2.0g	278.35	2.0g	279.03	>1
2.5g	307.54	2.5g	315.45	>1
3.0g	314.14	3.0g	329.84	>1
Number	120 Screen	Number	120 Screen	Washed/Unwashed
1.0g	189.88	1.0g	194.08	>1
1.5g	240.15	1.5g	241.60	>1
2.0g	268.66	2.0g	282.71	>1
2.5g	294.36	2.5g	301.38	>1
3.0g	321.25	3.0g	325.28	>1
Number	200 Screen	Number	200 Screen	Washed/Unwashed
1.0g	179.79	1.0g	200.65	>1
1.5g	230.98	1.5g	243.36	>1
2.0g	277.53	2.0g	284.91	>1
2.5g	305.15	2.5g	308.29	>1
3.0g	330.60	3.0g	335.84	>1

Sample and Particle Size

Coarse ground, fine ground, a number 60 screen, a number 120 screen, and a number 200 screen were used on 1.0 gram, 1.5 gram, 2.0 gram, 2.5 gram, and 3.0 gram samples. It is possible to compare the results by two variable analysis of variance. Since this analysis takes only the mean of the samples into consideration for comparisons the standard error is not included in the table.

TABLE II
Samples Compared in Counts per Minute

	Coarse	Fine	Number 60 Screen	Number 120 Screen	Number 200 Screen
Unwashed 1.0g	186.88	192.93	183.89	189.88	179.79
Unwashed 1.5g	238.54	236.61	245.98	240.15	230.98
Unwashed 2.0g	276.86	270.94	278.35	268.66	277.53
Unwashed 2.5g	301.56	299.74	307.54	294.36	305.15
Unwashed 3.0g	320.94	320.21	314.14	321.25	330.60
Washed 1.0g	194.76	198.62	197.92	194.08	200.65
Washed 1.5g	242.48	248.34	248.00	241.60	243.36
Washed 2.0g	270.48	285.48	279.03	282.74	284.91
Washed 2.5g	303.78	306.48	315.45	301.38	308.29
Washed 3.0g	317.92	333.55	329.84	325.28	335.84
		df	Mean Square		
Row means	58,058.56	9	6,450.95		
Column means	195.04	4	48.76		
Residual	57,379.54	36	1,593.87		
Total	115,633.14	49			

For the rows: $F = \dfrac{6{,}450.95}{1{,}593.87} = 4.04735$ $F_{95}(9, 30/40) = \dfrac{2.21}{2.12}$

Therefore we rejected the hypothesis that there was no difference in row means. There is a significant difference in the weights of the samples and the resultant count.

For the columns: $F = \dfrac{195.05}{57{,}379.54} = .003399$ $F_{95}(4, 30/40) = \dfrac{2.69}{2.61}$

Therefore we accepted the hypothesis that there was no difference in the column means. This demonstrates that the size of the particles has lettle effect on the specimen count.

Weight Increases of Samples

The following basic increases and percentage increases with weight were observed:

EFFECT OF SAMPLE PREPARATION 11

TABLE III

	Unwashed Coarse				Washed Coarse			
C/m		Increase	Per Cent of 1.0g	Percentage Increase	C/m	Increase	Per Cent of 1.0g	Percentage Increase
1.0g	186.88				194.48			
1.5g	238.54	51.66	127.64	27.64	242.48	48.00	124.50	24.50
2.0g	276.86	38.32	148.14	20.50	270.52	28.04	138.89	14.39
2.5g	301.56	19.38	161.36	13.22	303.78	33.26	155.97	17.08
3.0g	320.94	19.38	171.73	10.37	317.92	14.14	163.23	7.26
	Unwashed Fine				Washed Fine			
1.0g	192.93				198.62			
1.5g	236.61	43.68	122.64	22.64	248.34	49.72	125.03	25.03
2.0g	270.94	34.33	140.43	17.79	285.48	37.14	143.73	18.70
2.5g	299.74	28.80	155.36	14.93	306.48	21.00	154.30	10.57
3.0g	320.21	20.47	165.97	17.99	333.55	27.07	167.93	13.63
	Unwashed Number 60 Screen				Washed Number 60 Screen			
1.0g	183.89				197.92			
1.5g	245.98	62.09	133.76	33.76	248.00	50.08	125.30	25.30
2.0g	278.35	32.37	151.36	17.60	279.03	31.03	140.98	15.68
2.5g	307.54	29.19	167.24	15.88	315.45	36.42	159.38	18.40
3.0g	314.14	6.60	170.83	3.59	329.84	14.39	166.65	7.27
	Unwashed Number 120 Screen				Washed Number 120 Screen			
1.0g	189.88				194.68			
1.5g	240.15	50.27	126.47	26.47	241.60	47.52	124.48	24.48
2.0g	268.66	28.51	141.48	15.01	282.74	41.14	145.68	21.20
2.5g	294.36	25.70	155.02	13.54	301.38	20.64	155.28	9.60
3.0g	321.25	26.89	169.18	14.16	325.28	23.90	167.60	12.32
	Unwashed Number 200 Screen				Washed Number 200 Screen			
1.0g	179.79				200.65			
1.5g	230.98	51.19	128.47	28.47	243.36	42.71	121.28	21.28
2.0g	277.53	46.55	154.36	25.89	284.91	41.55	141.99	20.71
2.5g	305.15	27.62	169.72	15.36	308.29	23.28	153.64	11.65
3.0g	330.60	25.45	183.88	14.16	335.84	27.55	167.37	13.73

	Washed		
	x̄ Increase	x̄ Per Cent of 1.0g	x̄ Percentage Increase
1.5g	49.69	125.96	25.96
2.0g	35.88	144.70	18.74
2.5g	27.06	158.73	14.03
3.0g	20.58	169.44	10.71

	Unwashed		
	x̄ Increase	x̄ Per Cent of 1.0g	x̄ Percentage Increase
1.5g	51.78	127.78	27.78
2.0g	36.02	152.93	25.15
2.5g	27.20	161.74	8.71
3.0g	19.76	172.32	10.58

	Washed		
	x̄ Increase	x̄ Per Cent of 1.0g	x̄ Percentage Increase
1.5g	47.60	124.12	24.12
2.0g	35.75	142.25	18.13
2.5g	26.92	155.71	13.46
3.0g	21.41	166.56	10.85

Thus, it can be determined that, while the total count increases with sample size, the amount of this increase decreases with each weight increment. This could be due to two different factors. It might be a function of the depth of the sample; that is, while there is a constant surface area for the radiation or emission of particles in all samples, the depth is variable. As the depth of the sample in the container increases, the ability of the beta radiation to penetrate the overlying material decreases. This effect is probably offset to some degree by back-scattering. The gradual lag in increase also could be due to a mechanical loss of counts as the activity of the sample increases. It has been noted that two small sample counts may total more than the count of the combined amounts; with levels of 200 counts per minute and above there is a strong chance that on Crane's counter the emission of two beta particles may be registered as one count.

A percentage increase over the count of a 1 gram sample weight was also calculated. This was done to determine predicability of count increases with an increase in sample size.

It should be noted that the mean percentage increase to 1.5 grams is 125.96 with eight values falling within 3 per cent of the mean and all values falling within 6 per cent of the mean. For an increase in weight from 1.0 gram to 2.0 grams the mean percentage increase is to 144.70 per cent. Seven values fall within 4 per cent of the mean and all values fall within 7 per cent. With the larger samples the variation is less predictable. For an increase from 1.0 gram to 2.5 grams the mean percentage increase is to 158.73 per cent with eight values within 5 per cent, one value within 10 per cent and one value of 10.99 per cent. For an increase from 1.0 gram to 3.0 grams the mean increase is to 169.44 per cent with eight values within 5 per cent, one value within 7 per cent and one value of 14.44 per cent.

There is less mean percentage increase among the washed samples but this increase is apparently more regular.

Summary

The results of the PH2 series show that there is a significant difference between washed and unwashed samples, that there is no significant difference due to the size of the particles in the sample and that there is a predictable percentage increase in count with an increase from 1.0 gram to 3.0 grams.

Therefore, in succeeding runs an attempt was made to prepare washed samples of 1.0 gram or 1.5 grams. Because of the time involved in screening and the observation that screening made little difference the material was finely ground with no other special preparation technique.

THE EFFECT OF PARTICLE SIZE ON THE BETA ACTIVITY OF THREE SAMPLES OF MIXED COMPOSITION FROM RESEARCH CAVE, CALLOWAY COUNTY, MISSOURI

Charles F. Cleland and *Arthur J. Jelinek*
August 1962 (Revised March 1965)

Working with fossil ivory samples, Fitting has shown that there is no relationship between the level of beta activity and the grain size of a sample of uniform composition. The present series was undertaken to determine if these conclusions will hold for samples of mixed composition. That is, samples containing such diverse substances as bone, soil, charcoal, and organic debris. The samples were prepared by sifting through a 60-gauge wire screen and a 200-gauge silk screen, yielding four classes of samples: (1) unscreened, (2) material remaining on 60-gauge screen, (3) material remaining on 200-gauge screen, and (4) material passed through 200-gauge screen.

Sufficiently large quantities of material were used in the sifting process to retain a 1 gram sample after each screening.

The samples were run from the University of Michigan file of dated radiocarbon specimens: M-615, M-616 and M-617 from Research Cave, Missouri (Crane and Griffin, 1960: 36).

TABLE I

Phoenix—Memorial Number	C-14 Number	Beta Activity	Nature of Sample	Size
PH 12-5	M-616	9.43 ± .44	Soil, charcoal, bone	....
PH 12-6	M-615	10.39 ± .49	Soil, charcoal, bone	....
PH 12-7	M-617	9.77 ± .43	Soil, charcoal	....
PH 12-34	M-615	8.90 ± .34	Soil, bone, charcoal	>200
PH 12-35	M-615	10.93 ± .44	Soil, bone, charcoal	<200
PH 12-36	M-616	7.85 ± .32	Soil, bone, charcoal	> 60
PH 12-37	M-616	8.72 ± .37	Soil, bone, charcoal	>200
PH 12-38	M-616	9.97 ± .34	Soil, bone, charcoal	<200
PH 12-39	M-617	7.20 ± .34	Soil, charcoal	> 60
PH 12-40	M-617	8.85 ± .39	Soil, charcoal	>200
PH 12-41	M-617	10.56 ± .42	Soil, charcoal, alvar	<200
PH 12-43	M-617	6.57 ± .29	Soil, charcoal	> 60
PH 12-44	M-617	8.18 ± .32	Soil, charcoal	>200
PH 12-45	M-617	10.12 ± .41	Soil, charcoal	<200

EFFECT OF PARTICLE SIZE

The unsifted samples were first tested to determine whether they represented a single population:

	x	$(x-\bar{x})$	(s)	$(x-\bar{x})^2$	$(s)^2$
PH 12-6	10.39	.53	.49	.2809	.2401
PH 12-5	9.43	.43	.44	.1849	.1936
PH 12-7	9.77	.09	.43	.0081	.1849
				.4739	.6186

N = 3
$\bar{x} = 9.86$

$S_{\underline{a}}^2 = \dfrac{.4739}{2} = .2369$

$F = \dfrac{.2369}{.1756} = 1.35$

$S_{\underline{w}}^2 = \dfrac{.7027}{4} = .1756$

$F_{g5}(2,\text{inf}) = 2.99$

Thus the samples do not appear to be drawn from more than one population.

The same test applied to the materials which failed to pass through the 60-gauge screen indicates that here more than one population appears to be present.

	x	$(x-\bar{x})$	s	$(x-\bar{x})^2$	$(s)^2$
PH 12-36	7.85	.64	.32	.4096	.1024
PH 12-39	7.20	.01	.34	.0001	.1156
PH 12-43	6.57	.64	.29	.4096	.0841
				.8193	.3021

N = 3
$\bar{x} = 7.21$

$S_{\underline{a}}^2 = \dfrac{.8193}{2} = .4096$

$F = \dfrac{.4096}{.1007} = 4.06$

$S_{\underline{w}}^2 = \dfrac{.3021}{3} = .007$

$F_{95)}(2 \text{ inf}) = 2.99$

The material sifted through the 60-gauge screen and retained in the 200-gauge screen appears quite homogeneous.

PH 12-34	8.90	.24	.34	.0576	.1156
PH 12-37	8.72	.06	.37	.0036	.1369
PH 12-40	8.85	.19	.39	.0361	.1521
PH 12-44	8.18	.48	.32	.2304	.1024
				.3277	.5070

$N = 4$

$\bar{x} = 8.66$

$S_{\underline{a}}^2 = \dfrac{.3277}{3} = .1092$

$F = \dfrac{.1092}{.1267} = F = .86$

$S_{\underline{w}}^2 = \dfrac{.5070}{4} = .1267$

$F_{95}(3 \text{ inf}) = 2.60$

The material which passed through the 200-gauge screen also behaves as a single population.

	x	$(x-\bar{x})$	s	$(x-\bar{x})^2$	$(s)^2$
PH 12-35	10.93	.53	.44	.2809	.1936
PH 12-38	9.97	.43	.34	.1849	.1156
PH 12-41	10.56	.16	.42	.0256	.1764
PH 12-45	10.12	.28	.41	.0784	.1681
				.5698	.6537

$N = 4$

$\bar{x} = 10.40$

$S_{\underline{a}}^2 = \dfrac{.5698}{3} = .1899$

$F = \dfrac{.1899}{.1634} = 1.42$

$S_{\underline{w}}^2 = \dfrac{.6537}{4} = .1634$

$F_{95}(3 \text{ inf}) = 2.60$

It may thus be shown that there is a significant relationship between the grain size of samples of mixed composition and the amount of beta activity which they emit. The preceding tests show that there were no statistically significant differences in the beta activity within the groups of unscreened samples, samples which passed through only the 60-, and the 60- and 200-gauge screens. Inspection of the range of beta activity with each sorting also indicates that there is an inverse relationship between the level of beta activity and the grain size; that is, the

TABLE II

Unscreened	9.43 ± .44	....	10.39 ± .49
60-gauge wire screen	6.57 ± .29	....	7.85 ± .32
200-gauge silk screen	8.18 ± .32	....	8.90 ± .34
200-gauge silk screen	9.97 ± .34	....	10.93 ± .44

series appears to demonstrate that particles of larger size in these mixed samples are of less active materials. Most of the matter removed by the 60-gauge screen appeared to be charcoal and other organic debris. A single 1 gram specimen of pure bone from sample M617 was tested with a resulting count/minute of 627 ± 29; lower than any of the mixed samples tested. This and the results of the screening would indicate that the majority of activity in these specimens is due to minerals in fine soil particles rather than to minerals absorbed in bone or other organic materials. This would account for the lack of homogeneity in the material removed by the first screening since the irregular large particles of relatively inert materials would tend to hold varied amounts of fine soil particles.

It is also interesting to note that the relative order of the unscreened and < 200-gauge samples is consistent with the radiocarbon age of the samples; the oldest (M615 at 4770 ± 300 B.C.) showing the highest activity and the youngest (M616 at 4230 ± 300 B.C.) is intermediate in both age and activity (Crane and Griffin, 1960). While the magnitude of difference of neither the dates nor the gross radioactive samples is statistically significant it suggests that we are dealing with a time accumulation of radioactive material and that radiocarbon probably does not contribute significantly to the total activity of these specimens.

THE EFFECT OF DIFFERENTIAL CHARRING ON THE BETA ACTIVITY OF BONE FROM THE PECOS RIVER VALLEY, NEW MEXICO

Charles E. Cleland
June 1962

The following 1.0 gram samples were selected and prepared in order to test the effects of different degrees of charring on bone specimens. All bone was submitted by Jelinek and was from the same provenience unit, Trench Number 1, 8-10 inches, Site P4B, De Baca County, N. M.

TABLE I

Phoenix Number	Type of Bone	Degree of Charring	Counts Per Minute	Standard Error
PH 4-29	Antelope long-bone (cancelous)	Uncharred	1.17	± .12
PH 4-30	Antelope long-bone (compact)	Uncharred	.92	± .10
PH 4-31	Rabbit pelvis	Uncharred	1.89	± .06
PH 4-32	Rabbit pelvis (unwashed)*	Partially charred	2.19	± .17
PH 4-33	Rabbit metatarsals	Charred	1.29	± .05
PH 4-34	Rabbit ulna (unwashed)*	Calcined	1.10	± .11
PH 4-35	Rabbit pelvis	Partially charred	1.12	± .12
PH 4-36	Rabbit tibia	Calcined	1.38	± .14

*While these specimens were not washed prior to preparation they had been washed following excavation as a part of normal museum procedure and did not appear to differ from the other specimens after washing.

The F test was used to determine whether there was any significant variation within this series. This test resulted in the following groupings:

TABLE II

Phoenix Number	Counts per Minute	Degree of Charring
	Group 1	
PH 4-30	.92 ± .10	Uncharred antelope longbone
PH 4-34	1.10 ± .11	Calcined rabbit ulna
PH 4-35	1.12 ± .12	Partially charred rabbit pelvis
PH 4-29	1.17 ± .12	Uncharred antelope longbone
PH 4-33	1.29 ± .05	Charred rabbit metatarsals
PH 4-36	1.38 ± .14	Calcined rabbit tibia
	Group 2	
PH 4-31	1.89 ± .06	Uncharred rabbit pelvis
PH 4-32	2.19 ± .17	Partially charred rabbit pelvis

Although there were two significantly different groups in this series, these groups clearly have no relationship to the degree of charring. We must therefore conclude that within this sample, the degree of charring appears to have no significant effect on the beta activity of recent bone.

HEAT ALTERATION AND RADIOACTIVITY IN FOSSIL BONE

James E. Fitting

February 1963

Binford (1962:32) has suggested that heat alteration affects the capacity of bone to absorb radio-active elements from solutions in the soil. This premise was based on the work of Neuman, Neuman, Main, and Mulryan (1949) and Binford's own work on material from the Oconto site. Binford's paper has stimulated further research along these lines and some of the results of this research are given here.

In the preceding paper Cleland concludes that "the degree of charring appears to have no significant effect on the beta activity of recent bone."

In January of 1963 a series of samples were run in order to further examine the effect of heat alteration on the absorbtive qualities of bone. In this controlled series only two specimens were used; one was a human ulna and the second was a fragment of deer long bone, both from the Moccasin Bluff site, a late Woodland site in Berrien County, southwestern Michigan. These bone fragments were split lengthwise to include both interior and exterior surfaces in each half. One of the halves of each sample was charred over a Bunsen burner. The charred and uncharred bones were again split. One set of charred and uncharred deer and human bone was stored in a closed box while the other set was soaked in a matrix composed of sand, caliche, and pulverized bone and dentine from the grey sand level of Blackwater Draw Number 1 locality in New Mexico. Samples of bone from this locality ran consistently over 300 counts per minute, considerably higher than any samples from the Great Lakes area. The matrix and samples were covered by water which was allowed to evaporate before more water was added. The samples remained in this matrix from September of 1962 until January of 1963 when 1 gram samples were prepared from each of the bone fragments.

The results of the tests are given below. All values are voltage-corrected beta counts per minute and two runs were recorded for each sample.

TABLE I

	Human Ulna			Deer Longbone		
	Number	C/M	S.E.	Number	C/M	S.E.
			Charred			
Not soaked	PH 15-1	1.16 1.10	.06 .08	PH 15-5	.15 .57	.11 .05
Soaked	PH 15-2	13.23 14.56	.36 .40	PH 15-6	12.17 11.15	.30 .39
			Uncharred			
Not soaked	PH 15-3	1.25 1.03	.12 .06	PH 15-7	.36 .36	.10 .08
Soaked	PH 15-4	10.92 9.85	.37 .38	PH 15-8	13.37 14.21	.36 .32

A number of things can be noted from these results. It appears that charring makes no difference in the bone samples not subjected to the soaking process. The PH15-1 and PH15-3 runs were subjected to the F test and there was no significant difference between these samples. An attempt was made to group PH15-5 and PH15-7 in the same manner. Here a significant difference was found (F = 3.79; $F_{(3, inf.)99}$=3.78) but it is caused by the discrepancy between the runs of PH15-5. If we had averaged the runs instead of giving each separate run both PH15-5 and PH15-7 would be .36 counts per minute.

The samples which have been soaked in the matrix are all considerably more active than their unsoaked counterparts. For human bone the charred portion has a higher count than the uncharred portion. On the other hand, the reverse is true for the deer bone. This leads to the same conclusion reached by Cleland in his study of heat-altered and unaltered bone samples; that charring does not have a predictable effect on the absorbtive qualities of bone.

Thus, we must re-examine Binford's premise on the effect of charring. We established the following categories of heat alternation: (1) ashed, (2) calcined, (3) charred, and (4) partially charred. In Clelands' series all but the ashed category was present. In the PH15 series the bones were charred. Binford mentions Neuman, Neuman, Main, and Mulryan (1949) whose samples were "ashed," and a cremation from Oconto, which was probably calined or charred rather than "ashed" (Binford, 1962: 39), since the description specifically mentions skull fragments and long bones (Binford 1962: 35).

One problem appears to be the use of the term "ashed." In the article by Neuman and others, the bone was "ashed" by boiling in Alkaline glycol at 200 degrees. They state that "It was noted that bone preparations which had been ashed in alkaline glycol removed uranium from the bicarbonate buffer, whereas bone preparations ashed at a high temperature in a muffle furnace did not" (Neuman, Neuman, Main, and Mulryan, 1949: 336). They further noted that, "Within the limits of experimental error, the high temperature treatment completely prevented the transfer of uranium from buffer to bone," 1949: pp. 336-37. Thus, the ashed bone of their studies which did show a tendency to take up more uranium was very different from the heat altered bone in archaeological deposits, middens, and cremations.

The samples from the Oconto site do not furnish us with much information in this regard. Only one burial, represented by three samples, is heat altered. While Binford states that "It is certainly outside of the range of radiation exhibited by the compact long bone; . . . ." (1962: 39) it would appear that the beta counts of 2.49, 2.81, and 2.34 per minute would fall within the range of the samples of compact bone from Burial Number 2, Feature Number 1, Area II, which are 3.16 and 1.96 counts per minute. The last set was prepared from the same type of material as the cremation burial (skull and longbones). The heat-altered material from the Oconto site, then, does not appear to be an exception to our findings.

In summary, our evidence at present consists of two natural sites, Oconto and P4B, where heat-altered and unaltered bone both occur. In neither instance can heat alteration be consistently correlated with increased or decreased beta activity. In addition, we have two controlled laboratory studies; one, PH15, suggests that charring has no predictable effect, while the other, by Neuman, Neuman, Main, and Mulryan, suggests that intense heat alteration inhibited transfer of uranium to bone. On the basis of this information it would seem that heat alteration of archeological material will either not affect the absorbtion rate of naturally occuring radioactive elements or may, under extreme conditions, inhibit this absorbtion.

INTERNAL VARIATION IN RADIOACTIVITY OF A STANDARD SAMPLE

James E. Fitting
October 1962

An examination of sample counts on specimens run during 1961 and 1962 suggested that our techniques for computing sample count and, more particularly, standard errors might not accurately be reflecting the relationship between samples. In June of 1962, a series of fifteen samples of 1 gram weight were taken from a uniform preparation of washed, pulverized mammoth tusk. This was the same preparation used for Series PH 2 so we were able to anticipate the approximate level of the count (see p. 7).

Each of the fifteen samples was run through the counter five times, each run taking place on a different day. This gave us data to investigate the following problems: (1) variation between fifteen samples of the standard preparation; (2) variation between the five runs of the series; and (3) conformity of the computer standard error to the observed standard error of the sample means.

A preliminary examination of the values (Table I) suggested that there was more uniformity between sample runs than between runs of the same sample. The total count of the fourth runs is considerably higher than the totals of the other runs. Because we were concerned with two variables, individual samples and individual runs, a two variable analysis of variance was done on the data in Table I. We were able to gain the following information:

	Sum of Squares	Degrees of Freedom	Mean Square
Column means...	751.55	4	187.89
Row means.....	273.12	14	20.51
Residual.......	2,619.92	56	43.21
Total	3,644.59	74	

For the rows (variation between samples):

$$F = \frac{20.51}{43.21} = .47 \qquad F_{95}(14,56) = 1.88$$

It therefore appears that there is no significant difference between the fifteen samples of the standard mammoth tusk preparation.

For the columns (variation between runs):

$$F = \frac{187.89}{43.21} = 4.35 \qquad F_{95}(4.56) = 2.54$$

The runs show a statistically significant difference which, at first, was difficult to explain. Visual inspection of Table I suggested that this was primarily due to the increased counts in the fourth run. First, the voltage plateau was checked for the counter

TABLE I

Uncorrected Beta Count

PH Number	Run Number 1	Run Number 2	Run Number 3	Run Number 4	Run Number 5	Total
9-1 ...	179.58	179.82	183.87	189.15	187.37	919.79
9-2 ...	185.65	187.72	192.15	190.19	177.49	933.10
9-3 ...	186.61	180.88	181.20	188.94	189.12	926.75
9-4 ...	181.38	184.38	188.22	196.31	187.12	937.41
9-5 ...	175.49	177.64	181.81	188.23	184.32	907.49
9-6 ...	177.43	180.51	185.22	193.71	184.61	921.48
9-7 ...	179.60	176.71	185.42	191.88	181.50	915.11
9-8 ...	182.48	179.19	186.93	194.14	171.85	934.59
9-9 ...	180.85	187.62	185.82	190.19	181.80	926.28
9-10...	178.72	179.75	183.56	187.76	183.33	913.12
9-11...	185.07	189.23	186.64	189.94	190.70	942.58
9-12...	184.98	176.82	182.93	188.20	184.33	917.26
9-13...	182.39	179.96	177.14	190.34	189.76	919.59
9-14...	177.17	179.28	188.02	184.65	183.59	912.71
9-15...	185.79	181.42	183.53	189.40	183.64	923.78
Total ..	2,724.19	2,720.83	2,772.46	2,853.03	2,780.53	13,851.04

during the first part of June. No significant variation was noted in the records. Next the background was checked for this period. It was found that the background was low for the fourth run. It was 1.19 counts per minute as opposed to an average of about 1.25 counts per minute and a high for this series of 1.30 counts per minute. This however, would not account for the extreme variation between runs.

The remaining alternative was to check the voltage variation during this period. The method for making a correction for voltage variation was not used for samples running over 10 counts per minute, since the correction factor caused a great deal of distortion in the larger counts. For samples under 10 counts per minute the correction factor would vary from 1.05 to .95; for counts

INTERNAL VARIATION OF A STANDARD SAMPLE 25

as large as those in Series PH 9 it would vary between .31 and .38. A basic count of 200 beta emissions per minute, known to be an underestimate because of the efficiency loss of the counter in the higher ranges, would be further reduced to about 70 with the use of this correction factor. It does, however, correct for extremely large or small differences between uncanceled and total counts which reflects variation in voltage. All 75 values were re-computed and are given with their correction factors in Table II.

The relationships between the mean correction factors and the total uncorrected counts of the five runs are interesting. The total uncorrected counts for the first two runs (Table I) were 2,724.19 and 2,720.83. Their mean correction factors are .352 and .353 respectively. The total uncorrected counts for the third and fifth runs were 2,772.46 and 2,780.53 while their respective correction factors were .349 and .346. For the fourth run with a total of 2,853.03 the correction factor was .337, thus there is a near perfect inverse relationship between the size of the total count of the runs and the necessary correction factor.

It is therefore apparent that the population is statistically homogeneous, a situation which we know is in accord with reality.

Our final area of inquiry has to do with the relationship of the standard error computed for each sample to the standard error of the means of the observations. In performing the analysis of variance we collected all data necessary for finding the standard errors of the values in Tables I and II.

For the uncorrected count we have the following data:

$$s^2 = \frac{Sx^2 - \frac{(Sx)^2}{n}}{n-1} = \frac{2,561,662.04 - 2,558,017.45}{74} = 49.2512$$

$$s = \sqrt{s^2} = \sqrt{49.2512} = 7.02$$

For the corrected counts we have, in a sense, coded our data in preparing the problem. $S(x - \bar{x}) = Sx = 0$ in our coded problem while $S(x - \bar{x})^2$ gives us Sx^2. It follows that:

$$s^2 = \frac{314.9508 - 0}{74} = 4.2561 \qquad s = \sqrt{s^2} = \sqrt{4.2561} = 2.06$$

The mean of the standard errors computed for the individual samples is 2.97 counts per minute. Since the s value of the corrected and uncorrected counts per minute assumes a normal distribution of means, the standard error of each sample, being based on a Poisson distribution with a time correction, is not directly comparable. The very expression, "mean of standard

TABLE II
Corrected Beta Count
C.F. = Correction Factor

PH Number	Run Number 1	Run Number 2	Run Number 3	Run Number 4	Run Number 5	
9-1	64.72	66.55	62.52	62.42	58.08	
c.f.	.36	.37	.34	.33	.31	x̄c.f.R. #1
9-2	66.83	66.04	65.33	63.76	67.45	.352
c.f.	.36	.33	.34	.33	.38	
9-3	65.31	63.31	65.23	66.12	64.30	
c.f.	.35	.35	.36	.35	.34	x̄c.f.R. #2
9-4	63.48	66.38	62.11	64.78	63.62	.353
c.f.	.35	.36	.33	.33	.34	
9-5	63.17	63.95	63.63	64.00	64.50	
c.f.	.36	.36	.35	.34	.35	x̄c.f.R. #3
9-6	62.10	63.18	62.97	65.86	64.81	.349
c.f.	.35	.35	.34	.34	.35	
9-7	64.66	63.62	64.90	65.20	65.34	
c.f.	.36	.36	.35	.34	.36	x̄c.f.R. #4
9-8	62.04	62.72	65.43	67.95	65.23	.337
c.f.	.34	.35	.35	.35	.34	
9-9	61.49	65.67	59.46	62.76	67.26	
c.f.	.34	.35	.32	.33	.37	xc.f.R. #5
9-10	60.76	64.71	64.25	61.96	64.17	
c.f.	.34	.36	.35	.33	.35	
9-11	63.26	66.23	67.19	62.68	66.75	
c.f.	.34	.35	.36	.33	.35	
9-12	64.74	61.89	64.03	63.99	64.52	
c.f.	.35	.35	.35	.34	.35	
9-13	65.66	62.99	67.31	59.00	60.72	
c.f.	.36	.35	.38	.31	.32	
9-14	65.55	62.75	67.69	64.63	62.42	
c.f.	.37	.35	.36	.35	.34	
9-15	65.03	63.50	66.07	68.18	62.44	
c.f.	.35	.35	.36	.36	.34	

errors" is statistically meaningless. We can say, however, that the standard errors computed for each sample on the assumption of a Poisson distribution ($\bar{x}$ = 2.97) is closer to the standard error of the means of the corrected count (2.06) than to that of the means of the uncorrected counts (7.02).

In conclusion we may return to our three original problems and make the following statements:

1. Variation between samples is within predictable limits using both the uncorrected and corrected counts.

2. Variation between runs is within predictable limits provided counts are corrected for variation in voltage.

3. The standard errors computed on the basis of a Poisson distribution appear to reflect the variation of the corrected count more accurately than that of the uncorrected count.

The following suggestions are made for future research on the basis of this study of variation: (1) All statistical comparisons should be made on the corrected count even though there is distortion of the count size in making this correction. (2) All nonstatistical comparisons of the material run at different periods of time, whether days, months, or years, should be made on the basis of corrected count. (3) Comparisons made on the basis of uncorrected count should be viewed as indicative and not absolute unless the series is fairly homogeneous and run over a short period of time.

PART II

RADIOACTIVE ASSAY OF BONE MATERIALS FROM THE RIVERSIDE CEMETERY, MENOMINEE COUNTY, MICHIGAN

Lewis R. Binford
May 1959

Previous experiments on the adsorptive properties of bone indicated that human bone exposed in a quartz sand environment at the Andrews site, Saginaw County, Michigan, did not adsorb radioactive minerals over a period of some three thousand years (Binford, 1962). The Riverside Cemetery is located in Menominee County, Michigan, on a prehistoric beach where the sand environment is quite similar to that at the Andrews site. Two carbon-14 dates were obtained on human bone from burials at the Riverside Cemetery. One yielded a date of A.D. 650±200 (M-772, Crane and Griffin, 1964) and the other M658, was 1090±300 B.C. (Crane and Griffin, 1960). The discrepancy between the two dates as well as the possibility of a later occupation at the site (pottery was found on the surface) provided an excellent situation for both testing and the previous findings about the adsorptive properties of bone and possibly adding some information about the chronology of the occupation.

The following specimens were selected for testing:

TABLE I

Specimen		Run Number 1 C/M	Run Number 2 C/M
M4-1	Human cremated bone from feature number 7	1.12	1.38
M4-2	Human cremated bone from feature number 2	.83	.68
M4-3	Human cremated bone from feature number 10 C-14 dated at 1300 B.P.	3.34	3.58
M4-4	Human cremated bone from feature number 4	.79	1.04
M4-5	Deer bone from test pit	.41	.55
M4-6	Human cremated bone from feature number 6 C-14 dated at 3040 B.P.	.86	.72

The basic question that we are concerned with answering here, is whether all the above samples can be considered to represent a single population with respect to beta emissions. In order to solve this question an analysis of variance was calculated comparing the two runs on each sample against the variation between each sample. The results are given below.

(1) Within and among sample variance for the above specimens:

Series	Degrees of Freedom	Variance
Between sample	5	12.08
Within sample	6	.19
Total	11	12.27

A value of 63.58 was obtained for (F) which is far in excess of the 8.75 expected at the 1 per cent level of probability. From this I conclude that there is, in fact, more than one population represented in the above series of specimens. Visual inspection of the specimen estimates shows that specimen M4-3 has a higher beta count than the other specimens. This is the specimen dated at 1300 B.P. Another specimen M4-5, which is a deer bone specimen, is exceedingly low. With regard to the latter case, other experiments have indicated that human bone and animal bone may adsorb radiation at differential rates. A calculation of variance for the series means without the M4-5 specimen indicated that more than one population was still represented in the series. A further calculation of variance was made on the series after M4-3 was eliminated. The selection of this specimen for elimination was made solely on the basis of its observed high count. The results are given in the following table:

(2) Within and among sample variance for the series after M4-3 and M4-5 were omitted:

Series	Degrees of Freedom	Variance
Between sample	3	.31
Within sample	4	.14
Total	7	.45

A value of 2.21 was obtained for (F) which does not exceed 6.59, the value expected at the 5 per cent level of probability. From this I conclude that only a single population is represented by specimens M4-1, 2, 4, and 6.

It would appear that M4-5, the deer bone specimen, exhibits a different radiation profile than do the human bone specimens.

Further experiments are necessary to determine the exact meaning of this observation, but if it turns out that radioactive particles are adsorbed differentially as a function of the differential properties of bone between animal species then consideration of this variable is necessary in the utilization of this technique to solve problems of intrusion versus inclusion.

The series of specimens M4-1, 2, 4, and 6 appear to represent a single population with regard to beta radiation emissions. M4-6 is the specimen dated by carbon-14 at 1090 B.C. This was a burial containing socketed copper points, tanged copper points, copper awls, beaver tooth knives, an arrow shaft straightener, and three flint projectile points. The other burials in the series appear to be typologically similar to the dated burial. This would tend to confirm the association indicated by the radiation data. The means of the two runs for the four specimens are:

 M4-1 . . . . 1.25 counts per min.
 M4-2 . . . . .75 counts per min.
 M4-4 . . . . .91 counts per min.
 M4-6 . . . . .79 counts per min.

The mean count for the above four samples is .93 counts per minute. This is slightly above the mean of .71 counts per minute for the samples from the Andrews site that, as it was mentioned previously, had a similar environment and dated at 1220 B.C. which is very close to the date on specimen M4-6. Calculation of variance for the series from the two sites indicated that they were not significantly different, and that they both can reasonably be considered a single population with regard to beta emissions. This supports the view that bone does not adsorb radioactive particles in a quartz sand and is a strong support for the relative contemporaneity of the two sites as indicated by the carbon-14 analysis.

The high count observed in specimen M4-3 is difficult to explain. It will be recalled that this is the specimen dated at A.D. 650 which certainly indicates that this burial was later than the others. The fact that the beta count is higher than for the specimens believed to be older is apparently contradictory to the theory of adsorption with which I have been operating. Normally I would interpret a higher radiation count as indicative of greater age. This anomaly is at present not understood and makes further experimentation imperative to determine the source of the observed descrepancy.

Conclusion

This experiment was originally designed as a test of the findings at the Andrews site. Two specimens, M4-5 and M4-3, were not observed to fit the expected pattern if the information supplied by the Andrews site experiment was complete. At present three possible situations have been suggested by these samples that were heretofore not considered: (1) the possibility that bone from different animal species adsorbs radiation differentially; (2) the possibility that the primary radiation in bone is relatively high and decreases with time, and (3) the primary radiation in bone from different animal forms is different, thus the radiation profiles at any given period after death, other things being equal, would be different. Of course the possibility that the carbon-14 dates are incorrect is always pertinent but must only enter into the interpretation of observed data after experiments have exhausted the possible explanations from the standpoint of this technique.

RADIOMETRIC ANALYSIS OF BONE AND SOIL MATERIAL FROM LLOYD'S ROCK HOLE, BEDFORD COUNTY, PENNSYLVANIA

Lewis R. Binford
December 1960

Radiometric determinations have been made on a total of twenty-four specimens from Lloyd's Rock Hole (twenty bone and four soil specimens). This material was submitted for analysis in March, 1960, by Dr. John E. Guilday, Carnegie Museum, Pittsburg, Pennsylvania. Dr. Guilday's report has been issued (Guilday, 1964). The catalogue and data sheets for the several specimens constitute Tables I to VI, below.

Beta radiation measurements were made on the various specimens in an attempt to determine whether the stratigraphic succession of bone materials in the sinkhole was evidence for the deposits having been accumulated over an extended period of time or relatively quickly. If the former was the case, it would be expected that beta radiation, measured in counts per minute, would be higher for bone specimens recovered from the deepest deposits while lower beta counts would be characteristic of the deposits closer to the surface. Study of the distribution of bone samples in the deposits in terms of their measured beta counts could also possibly provide a basis for inferring something about the hydrological history of the deposit.

All beta measurements were made under standardized conditions. Conversion of all the observed specimen counts was made with respect to a standard for voltage regulation of twenty-five cosmic ray counts per minute (the mean for cosmic rays observed over a six-year period). Corrections were made for background counts in terms of the mean of the observed background runs recorded during the period that the specimens were being measured (1.21 counts per minute). The results of the measurements of beta radiation are given in Table I.

It had been observed previously that soft, spongy bone tended to take up radioactive materials from its environment more readily than did hard, compact bone. For this reason the specimens of long bone were treated as one sample and the specimens of vertebra were treated as another. Table II presents the specimen estimates for long bone from levels 15, 16, 17, 18,

TABLE I
Lloyd's Rock Hole Catalogue of Specimens

Project Number	Original Number	Specimen Composition	Species	Depth	Count
M7-1 ...	CM 5522	4 vertebra	Lepus americanus	16 ft.	4.49
M7-1-2..	CM 5522	4 vertebra	Lepus amer.	16 ft.	6.62
M7-1-3..	CM 5522	1 long bone	Lepus amer.	16 ft.	3.65
M7-1-4..	CM 5522	1 long bone	Lepus amer.	16 ft.	4.85
M7-2 ...	CM 5526	1 long bone	Lepus amer.	19 ft.	4.28
M7-2-2..	CM 5526	1 long bone	Lepus amer.	19 ft.	4.36
M7-2-3..	CM 5526	1 long bone	Lepus amer.	19 ft.	4.80
M7-3 ...	CM 5495	3 vertebra	Lepus amer.	17 ft.	7.70
M7-3-2..	CM 5495	1 long bone	Lepus amer.	17 ft.	4.15
M7-3-3..	CM 5495	1 long bone	Lepus amer.	17 ft.	4.80
M7-4 ...	CM 5508	3 vertebra	Lepus amer.	15 ft.	5.82
M7-4-2..	CM 5508	1 long bone	Lepus amer.	15 ft.	2.90
M7-4-3..	CM 5508	1 long bone	Lepus amer.	15 ft.	4.52
M7-4-4..	CM 5508	1 long bone that articulates with M7-4-3	Lepus amer.	15 ft.	3.86
M7-5 ...	CM 5519	3 vertebra	Lepus amer.	10 ft.	6.54
M7-5-2..	CM 5519	2 long bones	Lepus amer.	10 ft.	4.68
M7-5-3..	CM 5519	2 ribs and 1 scapula	Lepus amer.	10 ft.	3.56
M7-6 ...	CM 5520	1 long bone	Lepus amer.	18 ft.	3.78
M7-6-2..	CM 5520	1 long bone	Lepus amer.	18 ft.	3.96
M7-6-3..	CM 5520	1 long bone	Lepus amer.	18 ft.	4.84
M7-7 ...	.....	clay sample	.....	20 ft.	16.64
M7-7-2..	.....	clay sample	.....	20 ft.	16.26
M7-7-3..	.....	clay sample	.....	20 ft.	17.19
M7-7-4..	.....	clay sample	.....	20 ft.	17.27

and 19 together with the appropriate information for the calculation of within and between sample variance as a test of the homogeneity of the population from which the samples were taken. An analysis of within and between sample variance was calculated. By dividing the "among sample variance" by the "within sample variance" we arrive at a value of 2.51 for (F). Testing the null hypothesis that all five samples were not drawn from a single population, we could expect an (F) value as large as that obtained to arise by chance more than five times in a hundred if in fact all five samples had been drawn from a single population. We can then reject the null hypothesis and assert that all five samples were in all probability drawn from a single population. Stated another way, we would expect that the variation observed among the sample means to arise simply as a result of sampling vagaries in more than five out of a hundred samples which were drawn from the same population.

TABLE II

	Level					Total
	15	16	17	18	19	
	x_1	x_2	x_3	x_4	x_5	
	Specimen Estimates (C/M)					
	2.90	3.65	4.15	3.78	4.28	....
	4.52	4.85	4.80	3.96	4.36	....
	3.86	....	....	4.84	4.80	....
Sx	11.28	8.50	8.95	12.58	13.44	54.75
N	3.00	2.00	2.00	3.00	3.00	13.00
$(Sx)^2$ ..	127.24	72.25	80.10	158.26	180.63	2,997.56
Sx^2 ...	43.74	36.85	40.26	53.40	60.37	234.62
$\frac{(Sx)^2}{N}$ ..	42.41	36.12	40.05	52.75	60.21	230.58
$\bar{x}$	3.76	4.25	4.47	4.17	4.48	21.13
s	.81	.85	.45	.57	.28	....

As a check on the possibility that there was a trend in the data, such as an increase in sample means with depth of deposit, a simple sign test utilizing the binomial expansion was calculated. The data for this test is given in Table III. It may be seen that out of five observations four of the signs are plus and only one is negative. By expanding the binomial $(q + p)^5$ we find that there are six possible arrangements of signs having one or less minus signs, out of the possible thirty-two arrangements of plus signs and minus signs. To calculate the probability of obtaining an arrangement as good or better than that observed simply by chance, six is divided by thirty-two which reveals that in as many as nineteen out of a hundred samples we would expect to obtain an arrangement as good or better than that observed purely by chance. Thus there appears to be no justification for ascribing any trend to the observed sample means.

Since the variance analysis indicates that the samples were probably drawn from a single population and the sign test indicates that there is probably no directional trend in the sample means, some information may be obtained from a knowledge about

TABLE III

Level	15	16	17	18	19
Mean count	3.76	4.25	4.47	4.17	4.48
Sign	plus	plus	plus	minus	plus

the population being sampled as estimated from the combined samples. The first question to be solved is to determine if the population being sampled is distributed normally with respect to beta count. In order to answer this question a simple curve-fitting problem was set up using grouped data. The expected numbers were calculated using the table of areas under the normal curve. The necessary information is given in Table IV. By consulting a table of chi square for the appropriate degrees of freedom we find that we would expect a value of chi square as large as that observed to arise as a result of sampling vagaries more than twenty times in a hundred. On the basis of this information we must conclude that a normal distribution is most probably represented by the sample.

TABLE IV

Observed and Expected Frequencies for the Distribution of Long Bone Samples from Levels 15-19 under the Hypothesis of a Normal Distribution

Class in Counts per Minute	Observed Frequency (o)	Expected Frequency (e)	Difference (d)	d^2	d^2
........3.5	1	1.20	.20	.04	.03
3.5 .... 4.0	4	3.23	.77	.59	.18
4.0 .... 4.5	3	4.31	1.31	1.72	.40
4.5 .... 5.0	5	2.88	2.12	4.49	1.56
5.0	0	.88	.88	.77	.88

Degrees of freedom = 2; chi square = 3.05.

The form of the observed distribution is interesting in that the mean is 4.21, median 4.28, and mode 4.80. A definite negative skew is indicated for the distribution which is best described by gamma, calculated from the second and third moments of the sample. In this case, gamma was found to have a value of -.50 which indicates a negative skew. By taking into consideration the relative inaccuracy of the sample for estimating the distribution of the parent population, we can make a better estimate of the skew of the population by multiplying beta prime by the reciprocal of (n) for the sample. This calculation yields a value of -.02 as the estimated beta prime of the population and hence a gamma value for the population of -.14 (gamma is the square root of the beta prime). The corrected gamma value still indicates a negative skew for the population being sampled. Inspection of the standard deviations of the samples from each level (Table I) reveals that the values of (s) are higher for the levels nearer the surface. Although the sample size is so small that very little confidence can be placed in either the gamma values or the (s) values, the concurrence of the two observations may indicate that the rate of deposition was not even throughout the accumulation of the deposit. It has been found that skewed curves are generally associated with deposits which have been affected by some event causing a differential deposition either in numbers or kind to the accumulated materials. Larger (s) values are associated with mixed deposits. For instance, deposits of cultural material that have been disturbed tend to show a positive skew in the upper levels where bone from lower deposits has been brought up and a negative skew in lower levels where bone from the upper deposits has been mixed with the mass of material deposited at an earlier time. Relatively unmixed levels exhibit a normal (I) curve and relatively lower standard deviations.

    The best interpretation of the bone from Lloyd's Rock Hole seems to be that for the levels 15 through 19 a single population is represented which is normally distributed with respect to the acquired radioactive particles as reflected in gross beta count. This probably also includes the deposits from level 10 on down, but there was only a single long bone specimen from level 10 which hardly constitutes an adequate sample. Nevertheless, it had a beta count of 4.68 counts per minute which is between the mode and the median of the sample distribution for levels 15 through 19. The value of 3.56 was obtained on a combined sample of ribs and a scapula. This also is comfortably inside the range of long bone samples so there seems to be no reason for not extending this interpretation to include up as high as level 10. Because of the relatively low standard deviation, .58 for the combined samples from levels 15-19, the inference that the deposit from layer 15 through 19 was accumulated in a relatively short period of time and has experienced a similar hydrological history since deposition seems justified. The form of the observed distribution of beta counts (negatively skewed (I) curve) is such that a differential rate of accumulation may be indicated. It is my impression that the accumulation was more rapid during the initial period of deposition and that possibly there was diminished accretion to the deposit for a period at least as long as that required for the accumulation of the mass of the deposit. Beta determinations on a much larger sample of bone from each layer could possibly confirm or refute this impression.

As mentioned previously it has been observed that soft, spongy bone tends to take up radioactive materials from its environment more readily than does hard, compact bone. The samples from Lloyd's Rock Hole afforded a good opportunity to test the validity of this observation. Eleven bone samples were from the same species and there were both vertebra (cancellous tissue) and long bones (compact bone) from each of four different levels (levels 10, 15, 16, and 17). The measured beta radiation of the long bone specimens had indicated that a single population was represented. Therefore, unless the two types of bone adsorbed radioactive particles differentially there was no reason to suspect that the vertebra would exhibit radiation counts of a different order than that observed for the long bone specimens.

In order to test the null hypothesis that the long bone and vertebra do not represent samples from different populations, a within and between sample analysis of variance was carried out (Table V).

The variance analysis reveals that there are less than one out of a hundred chances that the observed differences between the two samples could arise as a result of sampling vagaries if they were in fact drawn from a single population. We are justified in asserting with a high degree of confidence that they do represent two distinct populations with respect to radiation count. This demonstrates that different factors operate in soft, spongy bone as opposed to hard, compact bone with regard to the acquisition of radioactive particles from the environment.

In order to account for these findings, several factors were considered. It was thought that possibly because of the porous nature of the vertebra it was harder to clean them and that more clay and mud were included in the measured sample than was the case with the long bone specimens. To determine if this was a likely explanation, four samples of mud taken from level 20 were tested for beta count. The results of these runs are given in Table I. The mean count for the four specimens was 16.83 counts per minute. This is far in excess of any of the counts

TABLE V

Sample 1 Vertebra	Sample 2 Long Bone	Calculations		
		Sample 1		Sample 2
x_1	x_2	$S\Sigma x$	31.17	30.51
		n	5.00	7.00
6.54	4.68	x	6.23	4.36
5.82	4.52	$S\Sigma x^2$	199.92	134.34
4.49	3.86	$(S\Sigma x)^2$	971.57	930.86
6.62	3.65	$(S\Sigma x)^2$	194.31	132.98
7.70	4.85	n		
	4.15	s	1.18	.48
	4.80			

a) Calculation of among sample variance

$$S_a^2 = \frac{(S\Sigma x_1 + S\Sigma x_2)^2}{n_1 - n_2} - \frac{(S\Sigma x_1)^2}{n_1} + \frac{(S\Sigma x_2)^2}{n_2}$$

$$S_a^2 = \frac{(31.17 + 30.51)^2}{12} \quad (104.31 \; | \; 132.98)$$

$$S_a^2 = 10.25$$

b) Calculation of within sample variance

$$S_w^2 = \frac{S\Sigma(x_1)^2 + S\Sigma(x_2)^2 - \frac{(S\Sigma x_1)^2 + (S\Sigma x_2)^2}{n_1 \quad n_2}}{S\Sigma - k}$$

$$S_w^2 = \frac{334.26 - (194.31 + 132.98)}{10} + .697$$

c) Calculation of (F)

$$F = \frac{S_a^2}{S_w^2} = \frac{10.25}{.697} = 14.71$$

d) Degrees of Freedom

$$S_a^2 = 1 \qquad S_w^2 = 10$$

e) Probability

F at the .01 per cent level of probability of 10.04 for the appropriate degrees of freedom. Therefore, we may reject the null hypothesis for the observed value exceeds the expected value at the level of selected significance.

registered for the bone specimens, thus the presence of more mud in the vertebra was a possible explanation of the inflated counts observed for those specimens (6.23 C/m for the vertebra as opposed to 4.36 counts per minute for the long bone). In order to determine if this was the explanation for the inflated counts, each of the five vertebral specimens and the seven long bone specimens used in this experiment were (1) ashed to remove organic material, (2) treated with 33 per cent HCL to dissolve the inorganic bone material and (3) the solution was filtered through a (00) filter paper. The filter paper was dried and then weighed. The gross weights minus the weight of the filter paper is given in Table VI. All samples were of one gram of bone dust.

TABLE VI

Vertebra	Long Bone
.0023 gm.	.0022 gm.
.0021 gm.	.0026 gm.
.0025 gm.	.0023 gm.
.0022 gm.	.0023 gm.
.0023 gm.	.0025 gm.
	.0022 gm.
	.0023 gm.

It is obvious that there is no difference between the quantity of impurities included in the measured specimens of the two samples. At present the best explanation seems to be that the properties of the two types of bone are different with respect to the acquisition of radioactive particles.

The implication of this experiment is simply that not only do we have to control for the species but control must be obtained on the anatomical part of the given species that is used for comparative radiation studies. This would be particularly important when the study is designed to answer questions about the way in which deposits were accumulated or questions concerning the hydrological history of deposits.

Summary

The radiometric analysis of bone and soil specimens from Lloyd's Rock Hole has revealed that there is no real difference in the beta radiation characteristic of bone specimens from levels 15 through 19 (this also is probably true as high as level 10).

The distribution of the specimens of long bone from these levels was found to be a normal (I) curve with a negative skew. Although no conclusive demonstration was possible, this was interpreted as indicative of a slight shift in the rate of accumulation of the deposit, accumulation having occurred rather rapidly for the mass of the deposit with a diminished accretion over a period of time at least as long as that required for the original deposition of the mass of the deposit.

In addition to the findings relative to the interpretation of the deposits in Lloyd's Rock Hole, it was found that long bone and vertebra, both from *Lepus americanus* and taken from the same levels, represented distinct populations with respect to beta count. These findings were interpreted, at least for the time being, as indicative of differential absorptive properties for soft, spongy bone as opposed to hard, compact bone. These findings make it imperative that in further investigations designed for answering questions about the depositional or hydrological history of deposits specimens of the same species and preferably bones of the same anatomical part be used for the comparisons.

ANALYSIS OF BONE MATERIAL FROM THE
MEDICINE CROW SITE (39 BF2)
BUFFALO COUNTY, SOUTH DAKOTA

Lewis R. Binford
December 1960

In 1957 a series of samples from the Medicine Crow Site
(39 BF2) were submitted to the University of Michigan's Memorial—Phoenix Project Number 132 for radiation analysis by William N. Irving for the River Basin Surveys, Missouri Basin Project of the Smithsonian Institution. These specimens were analyzed by Arthur J. Jelinek, research assistant, then conducting the research. Jelinek summarized the results as follows:

> The study, then, indicates three separate deposits as concerns radioactive mineral deposition. The wide separation in level of activity of specimens in the lower two feet of the deposit indicates some sort of definite event, possibly a break in the cultural sequence, or equally possibly a stabilization of an evaporation table at this level for a considerable period of time. (Unpublished research report.)

During 1958 and 1959 the techniques for analyzing low-level bone specimens were modified and improved and it was thought that a reanalysis of the Medicine Crow material might add additional information to the earlier results. In November of 1959 a new series of bone specimens were requested and received from Mr. William N. Irving.

A total of thirty-five small long-bone fragments of an unknown species were prepared and analyzed for their radioactive properties. It has been shown (Binford, 1960) that bones of different species tend to absorb radioactive particles differentially; therefore, we can expect a relatively wide range of variation among specimens of essentially the same age if this sample was composed of bone from different species.

The results of the analysis are given in Table I.

Judging from the distribution of radiation in bone specimens from square J12-13 there would appear to have been four major periods of accumulation resulting in the observed cultural deposit. From the surface to a depth of around 1 foot (strata I) appears to be very recent deposits, probably accumulated within the

TABLE I

Depth Below Surface in Feet	Beta Emissions in Counts Per Minute by Square					
	Square I12-13	Square J12-13	Square J9	Square J10	Square K16-17	Square M13-14-15
.25–.50 ...	...	...	.70 .83	...	...	.74
.50–.75 ...	...	.40	...	...	...	2.46
.75–1.0 ...	...	...	...	...	...	...
1.0–1.25 ...	...	...	...	...	...	...
1.25–1.50 ..	...	1.80 1.53	...	...	...	...
1.50–1.75 ..	...	1.70	...	...	...	...
1.75–2.00 ..	...	1.48	...	...	...	...
2.00–2.25 ..	...	...	...	...	...	...
2.25–2.50 ..	4.54 4.90	...	...	...	...	...
2.50–3.00	4.61	...	...	...	...	...
3.00–3.25 ..	...	5.14 5.05	...	...	...	...
3.25–3.50 ..	...	5.64 6.33	...	...	...	...
3.50–3.75 ..	...	5.81	...	...	...	...
3.75–4.00 ..	...	5.29	...	...	...	...
4.00–4.25 ..	13.42 13.66	7.20	...	...	12.28 12.34	...
4.25–4.50 ..	...	5.17	...	...	...	...
4.50–4.75 ..	...	15.37 15.17	...	...	...	...
4.75–5.00 ..	21.90	13.64	...	...	...	...
5.00–5.25 ..	...	...	...	8.55 9.39	...	...
5.25–5.50 ..	...	...	...	...	...	...

historic period. From a depth of 1 foot to around 2 feet and possibly as deep as 3 feet (strata II), the deposit represents accumulations within the recent past, but probably separated from strata I by a period during which there were no accretions to the deposit. Below strata II, from a depth of 3 feet to approximately 4.5 feet, is strata III which was certainly deposited much earlier than the strata immediately above. Strata III appears to have accumulated relatively quickly, in that the bone specimens from the top of the strata do not exhibit radiation counts appreciably lower than the bone specimens from the bottom of the strata. Immediately underlying strata III is strata IV which must have been laid down at a much earlier date and separated from strata III by a long period during which either the deposit was eroding or during which there was little deposition of new material.

Bone specimens from other squares are of insufficient number to either confirm or refute the above interpretation. The information that the specimens from squares other than J12-13 do provide, is a hint that the depositional history of the site varies according to depth, that is, strata laid down at a given time are not at a uniform depth below the surface over the site. The samples from square I12-13 add confirmation to the positive correlation observed in square J12-13, of beta count with depth below the surface.

Jelinek suggested (see above) that the high counts observed for specimens from the lowest levels may reflect the point at which an evaporation table was stabilized. In view of the varying depth observed among the squares for the specimens having counts ranging from 12- to 20-counts per minute, it seems unlikely that the stabilization of the evaporation table is the variable involved.

An alternative hypothesis is that the lower levels were deposited at a relatively early time, followed by a long interval, during which the site was not occupied, and then at a much later period deposition was begun anew.

Summary

On the basis of such a small sample it is not possible to demonstrate meaningful differences both horizontally and vertically. Nevertheless, it has been suggested that the deposits at the Medicine Crow site were accumulated during four major periods of deposition, each being separated by periods of time during which there was either erosion or lack of deposition. Certainly the elapsed time between the deposition of strata IV and strata III was the greatest. Between strata III and strata II there was a much shorter period of time during which there was no deposition and between strata II and I there is the possibility that accumulation was continuous or at least with only a short time lapse between periods of deposition. Judging by the differences between squares in the correlation of beta count with depth, the depths below surface of the various strata vary considerably over the site. The reanalysis of the material has, in general, confirmed the results obtained by Jelinek, but the larger sample of materials has afforded the presentation of further interpretative information.

44 RADIOACTIVITY OF PREHISTORIC MATERIALS

TABLE II
Medicine Crow Site (39BF2) Catalogue of Specimens

Project Number	Cat. No.	Square	Depth	Species	Specimen Composition	Spec. Count	Time Min.	Uncorrected Spec. c/m	Observed Cosmic c/m	Result c/m
M8–1a	3679	I12–13	2.75–3.0	Unknown	bone scrap	769	119	6.46	28.08	4.54
M8–1b	3679	I12–13	2.75–3.0	Unknown	bone scrap	617	90	6.86	28.20	4.90
M8–1c	3679	I12–13	2.75–3.0	Unknown	bone scrap	1406	220	6.39	27.44	4.61
M8–2	2787	J12–13	0.50–0.75	Unknown	bone scrap	1851	1038	1.78	27.78	.40
M8–3a	3776	J10	5.00–5.50	Unknown	bone scrap	711	62	11.47	29.44	8.55
M8–3b	3776	J10	5.00–5.50	Unknown	bone scrap	853	70	12.18	28.74	9.39
M8–4	2791	J12–13	0.75–1.00	Unknown	bone scrap	Insufficient quantity				
M8–5a	3700	I12–13	4.00–4.50	Unknown	bone scrap	2490	143	17.41	29.82	13.42
M8–5b	3700	I12–13	4.00–4.50	Unknown	bone scrap	1037	60	17.28	29.12	13.66
M8–6a	3774	J9(F113)	.25–0.50	Unknown	bone scrap	429	205	2.09	27.46	.70
M8–6b	3774	J9(F113)	.25–0.50	Unknown	bone scrap	2017	890	2.26	27.67	.83
M8–7	2801	J12–13	1.75–2.00	Unknown	bone scrap	606	221	2.74	25.65	1.48
M8–8a	3807	J12–13	4.50–4.75	Unknown	bone scrap	2913	160	18.21	27.50	15.37
M8–8b	3807	J12–13	4.50–4.75	Unknown	bone scrap	2087	116	17.99	27.51	15.17
M8–9	2795	J12–13	1.50–1.75	Unknown	bone scrap	429	151	2.84	24.38	1.70
M8–10	4127	M13–14	0.50–0.75	Unknown	bone scrap	807	218	3.70	25.21	2.46
M8–11	3802	J12–13	4.25–4.50	Unknown	bone scrap	2538	378	6.71	26.36	5.17
M8–12a	2793	J12–13	1.25–1.50	Unknown	bone scrap	621	200	3.10	25.86	1.80
M8–12b	2793	J12–13	1.25–1.50	Unknown	bone scrap	544	189	2.88	26.39	1.53
M8–13	4124	M13–14	0.25–0.50	Unknown	bone scrap	1678	846	1.98	27.69	.74
M8–14	3793	J12–13	3.75–4.00	Unknown	bone scrap	1220	173	7.05	27.12	5.29
M8–15	2810	J12–13	1.75–2.00	Unknown	bone scrap	Insufficient quantity				
M8–16	2797	J12–13	1.75–2.00	Unknown	bone scrap	Insufficient quantity				
M8–17a	4052	K16–17	4.00–4.25	Unknown	bone scrap	1369	92	14.88	27.52	12.34
M8–17b	4052	K16–17	4.00–4.25	Unknown	bone scrap	1379	90	15.32	28.27	12.28
M8–18	3715	I12–13	4.75–5.00	Unknown	bone scrap	1930	76	25.39	27.66	21.90
M8–19	3790	J12–13	3.50–3.75	Unknown	bone scrap	805	116	6.94	24.74	5.81
M8–20	3799	J12–13	4.00–4.25	Unknown	bone scrap	1232	132	9.33	27.85	7.20
M8–21a	3809	J12–13	4.75–5.25	Unknown	bone scrap	2934	119	24.65	30.55	19.01
M8–21b	3809	J12–13	4.75–5.25	Unknown	bone scrap	873	50	17.46	29.36	13.64
M8–22a	3785	J12–13	3.00–3.25	Unknown	bone scrap	1074	165	6.51	26.08	5.05
M8–22b	3785	J12–13	3.00–3.25	Unknown	bone scrap	1323	192	6.89	27.18	5.14
M8–23a	3788	J12–13	3.25–3.50	Unknown	bone scrap	2499	301	8.30	26.77	6.51
M8–23b	3788	J12–13	3.25–3.50	Unknown	bone scrap	584	81	7.21	25.86	5.64
M8–23c	3788	J12–13	3.25–3.50	Unknown	bone scrap	655	87	7.53	25.37	6.33

REPORT ON THE RADIOMETRIC ANALYSIS OF ANIMAL AND FISH BONES FROM THE FEEHELEY SITE (20 SA 128), SAGINAW COUNTY, MICHIGAN

James E. Fitting
May 1962

The Feeheley site was brought to my attention by the excavator, Mr. David Taggart, who was anxious to determine whether the bones of small mammals and fish found in the excavation were contemporary with human burials from the site. The fact that many of these fragments were charred was cited as evidence of use by man. Mr. Charles Cleland, who was responsible for the identification of the bone material, considered the proportion of small fish and muskrat bones to reflect swampy conditions, probably during the time of the drop from the Nipissing Beach. If this were true, the animal and fish remains could represent a depositional situation earlier than, and unrelated to, the burial. A series of bone samples from the site were tested for level of beta activity to see if this method of analysis might shed light on the problem. The nature of the specimens and resultant counts are given in Table I.

The first step in our evaluation of beta activity was a comparison of specimens representing single excavation units (units 10-305, 30-300, 60-150).

For unit 10-305 three levels were represented with one sample from each level. Samples PH7-9, PH7-10 and PH7-11 portrayed the stratigraphic profile of this section. In addition, sample PH7-12 was a mixture of material from the three levels of this section. First, the difference between levels was tested:

Number	x	$(x-\bar{x})$	(s)	$(x-\bar{x})^2$	$(s)^2$
PH7-9	.74	.39	.08	.1521	.0064
PH7-10	1.17	.04	.05	.0016	.0025
PH7-11	1.47	.34	.19	.1156	.0361
				.2693	.0450

$N = 3 \quad \bar{x} = 1.13$

$S_{\underline{a}}^2 = \frac{.2693}{2} = .1346 \qquad S_{\underline{w}}^2 = \frac{.0450}{3} = .0153$

$F = \frac{.1346}{.0150} = 8.97 \qquad F_{95}(2.00) = 2.99$

TABLE I

Number	Nature	Location	Net Count	Standard Error
PH7-1	Human femur	70-400, sheet number 5-number 6, lower left of charcoal	.43	.09
PH7-2	Large mammal bone	From area of Peacock's surface collection	1.12	.10
PH7-4	Mammal bone (charred)	Test pit number 2, "fire pit"	1.06	.14
PH7-5	Mammal bone (charred)	30-300, below sod to sheet number 1	.57	.05
PH7-6	Human skull fragment	30-300, below sod to sheet number 1	.90	.11
PH7-7	Mammal bone (charred)	30-300, sheets number 1 - number 2	.48	.04
PH7-8	Mammal bone (charred)	5-315, surface - 3.0'	.57	.09
PH7-9	Mammal bone (charred)	10-305, surface to sheet number 1, -1.4 ± 2.2'	.74	.08
PH7-10	Mammal bone (charred)	10-305, sheet number 1 - number 2, 2.4' (flint area)	1.17	.05
PH7-11	Mammal bone (charred)	10-305, -2.8' -3.2'	1.47	.19
PH7-12	Mammal bone (part charred)	10-305, sheet number 1 - number 3, to -3.0'	1.04	.05
PH7-13	Mammal bone	60-150, surface-sheet number 1	.20	.11
PH7-14	Mammal bone (charred)	60-150, sheet number 2 - number 3, depth: 30"	.41	.13
PH7-15	Human bone (charred)	Feature number 2, Peacock's cremation	.14	.13
PH7-16	Human bone	Feature number 6	2.30	.23
PH7-17	Human bone	May 21 excavation, Feature number 1	2.66	.23
PH7-18	Human bone	Ossuary, Bois Blanc Island	.40	.13

Therefore, it appears that the three samples do not represent a single population.

When the highest and lowest pairs were tested for t we found that PH7-9 and PH7-10 were distinct (t = 4.55) and PH7-10 and PH7-11 were probably drawn from the same population (t = 1.53).

In order to compare these three samples with the mixed sample, the three runs were considered as separate runs on the same sample. The mean count per minute of PH7-9, PH7-10 and PH-11 is 1.13 with a mean standard error of .12. This mean standard error was compared with PH7-12 (1.04 ± .05) by means of the t test.

$$\sqrt{(.12)^2 + (.05)^2} = \sqrt{.0169} = .13$$

The difference is 1.13 - 1.04 or .09. This difference can be expressed in terms of standard errors as .09 ÷ .13 or only .69 standard errors which would be expected about 50 per cent of the time if they were part of the same population.

For 30-300 we had two levels for animal bone: (1) below the sod to sheet number 1 (PH7-5) and (2) sheet number 1 - number 2 (PH7-7). Here we also used the t test.

$$\sqrt{(.09)^2 + (.04)^2} = \sqrt{.0097} = .0985$$

.57 - .48 = .09   .09 ÷ .0985 = .9137 standard deviations

This result would be expected about 36 per cent of the time and furnished no basis for separating the two samples from this unit. It should be noted that the lesser activity is in the lower level; however as no exact provenience data was furnished and, since they appear to be part of the same population, they could have been adjacent to each other or separated by only a small vertical distance.

We had two mammal samples from 60-150 which were separated vertically; one from the surface to sheet number 1 (PH7-13), and the other in the area between sheet number 2 and sheet number 3 (PH7-14). The values are given and tested below:

$$\begin{aligned}
&\text{PH7-13} \qquad .20 \pm .11\\
&\text{PH7-14} \qquad .41 \pm .13
\end{aligned}$$

$$\sqrt{(.11)^2 + (.13)^2} = \sqrt{.0290} = .17$$

$$t = .41 - .20 \div .17 = .21 \div .17 = 1.24$$

This result would be expected in about 210 instances out of 1000 if the two samples were part of the same population. If we accept the 5 per cent level as significant these samples are accepted as part of the same population. It is important to note that there was more radioactivity recorded in the lower level, a situation in agreement with the 10-305 group.

Our next step was a comparison of mammal counts between excavation units. In addition to the units considered above, we had single specimens from 5-315 (PH7-8), Mr. Peacock's surface collection (PH7-2), and test pit number 2, "fire pit" (PH7-4).

Among the units with sequences of two or more levels there was no agreement between levels:

TABLE II

10-305	30-300	60-150
.74 ± .08	.57 ± .05	.20 ± .11
1.17 ± .05	.48 ± .04	.41 ± .13
1.47 ± .19		

On the basis of the cultural material from the site, it is probable that this lack of agreement is due to a difference in drainage or exposure. While we demonstrated that the two samples from unit 60-150 could be part of a single population, the deeper sample showed sufficient similarity to the 30-300 samples to warrant examination:

Number	(x)	(x-x̄)	(s)	(x-x̄)^2	(s)^2
PH7-5	.57	.08	.05	.0064	.0025
PH7-7	.48	.01	.04	.0001	.0016
PH7-14	.41	.08	.13	.0064	.0169
				.0129	.0210

$$N = 3 \quad \bar{x} = .49$$

$$S_{\bar{a}}^2 = \frac{.0129}{2} = .0064 \qquad S_{\bar{w}}^2 = \frac{.0210}{3} = .0070$$

$$F = \frac{.0064}{.0070} = .9122 \qquad F_{95}(2.00) = 2.99$$

Therefore these samples could be part of the same population.

We then grouped all samples from 30-300 and 60-150 and tested them for F:

Number	(x)	(x-x̄)	(s)	(x-x̄)^2	(s)^2
PH7-5	.57	.15	.05	.0225	.0025
PH7-7	.48	.06	.04	.0036	.0016
PH7-13	.20	.22	.11	.0484	.0122
PH7-14	.41	.01	.13	.0001	.0169
				.0746	.0332

THE FEEHELEY SITE

$N = 4 \quad \bar{x} = .42$

$S_{\bar{a}}^2 = \dfrac{.0746}{3} = .0248 \qquad S_{\bar{w}}^2 = \dfrac{.0332}{4} = .0083$

$F = \dfrac{.0248}{.0083} = 2.99 \qquad F_{95}(3.00) = 2.60$

This indicates a significant difference, so that what we may have is a sequence, with two overlapping components There is no possibility of an overlap of these samples with the samples from unit 10-305. Even when we considered the smallest of these values (PH 7-9) and tested it with the 30-300 samples it showed a significant difference:

Number	(x)	(x-$\bar{x}$)	(s)	(x-$\bar{x}$)^2	(s)^2
PH7-5	.57	.03	.05	.0009	.0025
PH7-7	.48	.12	.04	.0144	.0016
PH7-9	.74	.14	.08	.0196	.0064
				.0349	.0105

$N = 3 \quad \bar{x} = .60$

$S_{\bar{a}}^2 = \dfrac{.0349}{2} = .0175 \qquad S_{\bar{w}}^2 = \dfrac{.0105}{3} .0035$

$F = \dfrac{.0175}{.0035} = 5.00 \qquad F_{95}(2.00) = 2.99$

Therefore, we set off a distinct sequence with two subdivisions from unit 10-305

The single samples of mammal bone were then tested with the established groups. From Peacock's surface collection sample (PH7-2) we had a count of $1.12 \pm .10$. This was tested against PH7-10 by means of the t test:

$$\sqrt{(0.5)^2 + (.10)^2} = \sqrt{.0125} = .112$$

$$1.17 - 1.12 \div .112 = .05 \div .112 = .446$$

As expected, they appeared to be from the same population.

PH7-4, the sample from test pit number 2, "fire pit" with a value of $1.06 \pm .14$, was also shown to belong to this population. One other mammal bone sample was considered; PH7-8, 5-315, Surface to -3', with a count of $.57 \pm .09$. This appears to belong to the population from unit 30-300:

RADIOACTIVITY OF PREHISTORIC MATERIALS

Number	(x)	(x-x̄)	(s)	(x-x̄)^2	(s)^2
PH7-5	.57	.03	.05	.0009	.0025
PH7-7	.48	.06	.04	.0036	.0016
PH7-8	.57	.03	.09	.0009	.0081
				.0054	.0122

$N = 3 \qquad \bar{x} = .54$

$S_{\underline{a}}^2 = \dfrac{.0054}{2} = .0027 \qquad S_{\underline{w}}^2 = \dfrac{.0122}{3} = .0041$

$F = \dfrac{.0027}{.0041} = .6585 \qquad F_{95}\,(2.00) = 2.99$

Evaluation of Human Bone

The five samples of human bone examined appeared to represent at least four groups:

TABLE III

Number	Nature	Count	Standard Error
PH7-1	Femur	.43	.09
PH7-6	Skull	.90	.11
PH7-15	Cremation fragments	.14	.13
PH7-16	Burial, unidentified bone	2.30	.23
PH7-17	Burial, unidentified bone	2.66	.23

The only possible statistical grouping was between PH7-16 and PH7-17:

$$\sqrt{(.23)^2 + (.23)^2} = \sqrt{.1058} = .3253$$

$$t = 2.66 - 2.30 \div .3253 = .36 \div .3253 = 1.1066$$

Since this value would be expected about 280 times out of 1000 in the same population we consider that they represent one population.

It should be noted that PH7-16 was discolored by copper salts from artifacts accompanying the burial, while PH7-17 was not. Since PH7-16 had the lower activity of the two it would seem that

THE FEEHELEY SITE 51

minerals accompanying the copper salts could not be responsible for high activity level
It is still difficult to evaluate relationships between radioactive mammal and human bone The work done by Binford on the Riverside Cemetery material suggests that deer bone shows a lower count than human bone This appears to be further borne out by the Feeheley human bone and animal bone from the same unit (30-300) When this unit is tested for homogeniety the animal bone shows a significant difference from the human bone:

Number	Nature	(x)	$(x-\bar{x})$	(s)	$(x-\bar{x})^2$	$(s)^2$
PH7-5	Animal	.57	.08	.05	.0064	.0025
PH7-6	Human	.90	.25	.11	.0625	.0121
PH7-7	Animal	.48	.17	.04	.0289	.0016
					.0898	.0162

$N = 3$ $\bar{x} = .65$

$$S_a^2 = \frac{.0898}{2} = .0449 \qquad S_w^2 = \frac{.0162}{3} = .0054$$

$$F = \frac{.0449}{.0054} = 8.3148 \qquad F_{95}(2.00) = 2.99$$

In both instances mentioned above, the human bone has a higher count than the animal bone. An exception to this pattern is provided by the sample of human bone in this series from Bois Blanc Island, for which we have a count of .40 ± .13 (PH 7-18). This sample is from the Juntunen site and was found in what has been defined as Zone I of that site (Jelinek and Fitting, 1963). Mammal bone samples from this Zone at the site ran .90 ± .12 (PH3-38), .52 ± .09 (PH3-31), .83 ± .10 (PH3-41), .44 ± .05 (PH3-84), and .80 ± .09 (PH3-101). In all instances they had a higher count than the human bone.

Conclusions

There are two levels at which we might draw conclusions from this material—they might be referred to as the possible and the probable. The possible inferences are those dealing with comparisons of samples showing small, but statistically significant, differences. This high level of differentiation was used in the main body of this report, where it was shown that there were four groups of mammal bone and four of human bone. These were statistically defined populations and there was no correlation between the absolute activity of mammal and human bone. It should be borne in mind that our samples were small, and that the possibility of human error in excavation and interpretation was mentioned occasionally. When we add to this our lack of understanding of the processes governing the natural radioactivity of bone, we are forced to the conclusion that the above categories are, perhaps, only good possibilities.

In the larger view, we can observe some striking differences. We have specimens of mammal bone varying between .20 counts per minute and 1.47 counts per minute. Two human bone specimens fall within this range (PH7-7, .90: PH7-1, .43) and three fall outside of this range. The cremation is much lower than all other samples (PH7-15, .14), while the two burials, which are essentially alike in count, are much higher (PH7-16, 2.30: PH7-17, 2.66).

With the possible exception of the 30-300 samples it cannot be stated with certainty as to which human material the animal bone is associated. It would appear, however, that it is least likely that any mammal bone is associated with the burials and the occasional finds of human bone are more likely candidates for association. It can also be stated with some certainty, based on the findings of previous investigators, that the two burials examined are considerably older than the other bone material from the site, and that the cremation is somewhat younger.

THE BETA ACTIVITY OF HUMAN BONE FROM THE FEEHELEY AND ANDREWS SITES, SAGINAW COUNTY, MICHIGAN

Charles E. Cleland
July 1962

This series was designed in order to investigate several problems:
1). The usefulness of beta radiation in predicting the temporal relationship between two similar sites.
2). The difference in the amount of activity absorbed and united by different human skeletal elements.
3). The effect of red ocher and copper salts on the beta activity of bone.
4). The temporal range of the human burials within each site.

The Feeheley and Andrews sites were selected for this series because they are located in almost identical geological conditions, that is, on sand ridges of similar age which are located about 2 miles apart. The temporal relationship between the two sites is fairly well established with the Feeheley site dating between two occupations at the Andrews site (Feeheley M-1139; 1980 $\pm$ 300 B.C. and Andrews M-659; 1220 $\pm$ 300 B.C. and M-941, 3350 $\pm$ 300 B.C.). Both sites shared a complex of tightly flexed red ocher burials which was gradually replaced by crematory burials at the Andrews site. The Feeheley site burial complex appears to be of relatively short duration. Several specimens of bone from the Feeheley site are the same as those reported by Fitting in the preceding paper.

Table I is a list of the beta activity and provenience of each sample. The samples fall into two general groups as indicated in the table.

The first conclusion we can make about this series is that neither copper stains nor red ochre seem to correlate with the radiation. Second, the various skeletal elements used in this series do not seem to exhibit any real pattern in amount of beta radiation. One would expect that cancellous bone such as vertebrae would show a higher count than more compact bone such as long bone or ribs; this apparently is not the case as some of the highest and lowest samples were both ribs and vertebrae. There

TABLE I

Sample	Counts Per Minute	Site	Provenience	Element	Presence of Ochre and Copper Salts
Group I					
PH 11-8	.32 ± .07	F	Feature #2	Vertebra	Copper
PH 11-1	.32 ± .06	A	Feature #3	Cremation	Ochre
PH 11-10	.33 ± .04	F	Feature #1	Long bone	Ochre
PH 11-4	.38 ± .09	A	Pfeffier & Peacock	Vertebra	Copper
PH 11-5	.42 ± .06	F	Feature #8	Vertebra	Copper
PH 7-1	.43 ± .07	F	Sq. 70-400 SS 5-6	Femur	....
PH 11-9	.46 ± .07	F	Feature #7	Vertebra	Copper and ochre
PH 11-12	.50 ± .06	F	Feature #8	Rib	Copper and ochre
PH 11-2	.51 ± .08	A	Feature #11	Skull	None
PH 11-7	.61 ± .08	F	Feature #4	Long bone	Copper and Ochre
PH 11-13	.65 ± .08	F	Feature #8	Rib	Copper
PH 11-16	.70 ± .10	A	Pfeffier and Peacock	Long bone	Copper
PH 11-3	.70 ± .09	A	Feature #4	Rib	Copper
PH 11-14	.76 ± .09	F	Feature #2	Rib	Copper
PH 7-6	.90 ± .11	F	Sq. 30-300	Skull	....
PH 11-15	1.01 ± .09	F	Feature #12	Vertebra	Copper
Group II					
PH 11-6	2.29 ± .12	F	Feature #Q	Rib	Copper and ochre
PH 11-16	2.30 ± .23	F	Feature #6	Long bone	Copper
PH 7-17	2.66 ± .23	F	May 21 Feature #1	....	Ochre
PH 11-11	2.94 ± .19	F	Feature #6	Vertebra	Copper

appears to be a general correlation between the age of the specimens as shown by C-14 dates and the amount of beta activity which they exhibit. Both the C-14 dates and the cultural complexes at these two sites indicate that the Feeheley site predates the second occupation at the Andrews site. All but one of the

Andrews site samples belong to this later occupation. As might be expected, the beta activity shows an overlap between the two sites in the lower activity levels, with the most active Andrews site samples in the middle range of Group I. Group II is represented entirely by Feeheley site samples. Thus, on the basis of the beta activity alone it appears that the Feeheley site is indeed somewhat earlier than the later of the two Andrews occupations.

The date for the earliest Andrews occupation (3350 ± 300 B.C.) was obtained from charcoal thought to be associated with the poorly preserved remains of a skull (Feature number 11). The beta activity of a sample from this feature (PH 12-2) is quite low and falls in Group I. This is unexpected since two samples from Feature number 4 at the Feeheley site (PH 11-7 and PH 11-13) dated by Carbon-14 at 1980 ± 300 B.C., or approximately 1500 years later than the early Andrews occupation, both exhibited higher beta radiation than the sample from the early Andrews occupation.

This raises the question of the validity of the association of the Carbon-14 sample with Feature number 11. It appears that the only reason for associating the early Andrews Carbon-14 sample and Feature number 11 was their comparable depth. The bone from this feature was not preserved by copper salts and yet was recognizable as a skull, while other pre-Nipissing burials could be recognized only as tooth caps. The general condition of the skull was in fact quite similar to human bone from the upper levels of the Feeheley site. Therefore, the state of preservation, the questionable stratigraphic correlation, and the low beta radiation tend to indicate that at the Andrews site Feature number 11 may not be associated with the Carbon-14 sample.

An alternate hypothesis, based on inconsistency among the samples, is that low level beta radiation may not be an accurate indicator of age at these sites. The most striking inconsistency is shown in Feature number 1 at the Feeheley site, where one of two samples is placed low in Group I and the other in Group II. Since these two samples were excavated at different times of the year, however, there appears to be a possibility that they may not have been associated with a single feature.

BETA ACTIVITY OF THE ANIMAL BURIALS AT THE JUNTUNEN SITE (20 MK 1) ON BOIS BLANC ISLAND

Charles E. Cleland
June 1962

The only evidences of "ceremonial" activity at the Juntunen site, on the west end of Bois Blanc Island at Mackinac Island, were several animal burials, three of which are represented in Feature number 5, Sq. 1790-1185. These three were apparently interred at the same time and include a dog, an eagle, and a snowshoe hare, buried fully articulated in small pits at the three corners of a triangular-shaped soil discoloration. Although these burials occurred just beneath the surface they were associated with two small sherds which may belong to one of the earliest ceramic styles present at the site. Additional animal burials included an eagle from Feature number 28, Sq. 1700-1120, believed to be associated with soil horizon D (which appears to be somewhat earlier than Feature number 5), and a piece of bird long bone associated with a medicine bundle in Feature number 11 (a large ossuary). The final sample was a piece of bird long bone from Sq. 1700-1120, S.S. 9-10 which is associated with maize and falls between soil horizons D and E. This series was designed to test the temporal relationships between these apparently ceremonial features.

The corrected beta activity for the six samples is as follows:

TABLE I

PH No.	Provenience		Counts Per Minute	Standard Error
PH 3-110	Feature number 28 Sq. 1700-1120	Eagle burial	.58	$\pm$ .05
PH 3-111	Feature number 11 Bird bone from ossuary		.79	$\pm$ .05
PH 3-112	Feature number 5 1790-1185	Dog bone	.16	$\pm$ .06
PH 3-113	Feature number 5 1790-1185	Rabbit pelvis	.45	$\pm$ .09
PH 3-114	Feature number 5 1790-1185	Eagle bone	.32	$\pm$ .08
PH 3-115	Sq. 1700-1120 SS 9-10 Bird bone with corn		.61	$\pm$ .09

THE JUNTUNEN SITE

The F test was applied to see if the series represented more than one population:

	$\bar{x}$	$(x-\bar{x})$	(s)	$(x-\bar{x})^2$	$(s)^2$
PH 3-110	.58	.09	.05	.0810	.0025
PH 3-111	.79	.30	.05	.0900	.0025
PH 3-112	.16	.33	.06	.1089	.0036
PH 3-113	.45	.04	.09	.0016	.0081
PH 3-114	.32	.17	.08	.0289	.0064
PH 3-115	.61	.12	.09	.0144	.0081
				.3248	.0312

$N = 6 \quad \bar{x} = .49$

$S_{\bar{a}}^2 = \frac{.3248}{5} = .0649$

$S_{\bar{w}}^2 = \frac{.0312}{6} = .0052$

$F = \frac{.0649}{.0052} = 12.48$

$F_{95} - (5 \text{ int.}) = 2.21$

Therefore, it appears that more than one population is represented. Further testing for t and f has revealed the following meaningful groups:

TABLE II

	Counts Per Minute	Standard Error	Provenience
Group I			
PH 3-112	.16 ±	.09	Feature #5 Dog burial
PH 3-114	.32 ±	.08	Feature #5 Eagle burial
Group II			
PH 3-113	.45 ±	.09	Feature #5 Rabbit burial
PH 3-110	.58 ±	.05	Feature #28 Eagle burial
PH 3-115	.61 ±	.09	Sq. 1700-1120 SS 9-10 Bird bone with corn
Group III			
PH 3-111	.79 ±	.05	Feature #11 Bird bone from medicine bundle

While PH3-113 lies beyond the range represented by Group I its close relationship to PH3-114 is obvious.

The first general observation to be made about this series is that the counts as a whole are much lower than those published by Jelinek and Fitting (1963) for fish vertebrae from the same site. The difference may be due to the difficulty of removing excess soil from these vertebrae, which would contribute to a higher count The low amount of beta activity may also indicate that these animal burials are all associated with the latest occupations of the site, that is to say probably not earlier than horizon D.

Of the three groups, two of the three animal burials associated with Feature number 5, i.e., Group I seem to be the latest, as their proximity to the surface would indicate. The "early" sherds are thus either later than suspected or are not contemporaneous with these burials.

The second grouping tends to correlate the burials of Feature number 5 with the eagle burial of Feature number 28 and also to indicate that these two features are more or less contemporaneous with the late levels containing corn. Group III, the bird bone from the medicine bundle of Feature number 11, seems to be the earliest of the ceremonial artifacts by virtue of its higher activity level. It will be noted, however, that its count is not much higher than the other samples.

In summary, the low level of beta activity of these samples indicates that they are associated with the later occupations at the site, and probably all are included within the Late Woodland phases represented there.

REPORT ON THE BETA ACTIVITY OF FIVE BONE SAMPLES FROM THE PALEGAWRA SITE IN IRAQ

Charles E. Cleland
June 1962

This series consisted of five first phalanges of *Cervus elaphus* from the Palegawra Rock Shelter, Iraq (Braidwood and Howe, 1960:28-29). These samples were submitted by Robert J. Braidwood with data concerning their provenience within the site.

One gram of finely ground bone was run from each phalange. The following table lists the beta activity of each sample:

TABLE I

Phoenix Project No.	Oiriginal No.	Locality		Counts Per Min.	Standard Error
PH 10-1 ...	PB 13	E. Rear $\frac{1}{4}$	40-60 cm.	2.81	.19
PH 10-2 ...	P 418	W. Rear $\frac{1}{4}$	60-80 cm.	3.25	.20
PH 10-3 ...	PA5 and P73	Sq. 5	20-40 cm.	1.55	.13
PH 10-4 ...	PA2 and P167	Sq. 2	20-40 cm.	1.57	.14
PH 10-5 ...	PA3 and P107	Sq. 3	40-60 cm.	2.12	.09

An F test indicated that these counts represent more than a single population:

	x	$(x-\bar{x})$	(s)	$(x-\bar{x})^2$	$(x)^2$
PH 10-1	2.81	.55	.19	.3025	.0361
PH 10-2	3.25	.99	.20	.9801	.0400
PH 10-3	1.55	.71	.13	.5041	.0169
PH 10-4	1.57	.69	.14	.4761	.0196
PH 10-5	2.12	.14	.09	.0196	.0081
Totals				2.2824	.1207

$N = 5 \qquad \bar{x} = 2.26$

$S_{\underline{a}}^2 = \dfrac{2.2824}{4} = .5706 \qquad F = \dfrac{.5706}{.0241} = 23.76$

$S_{\underline{w}}^2 = \dfrac{.1207}{5} = .0241 \qquad F_{95}(4, \text{inf.}) = 2.37$

The samples with the three highest counts also appear to represent more than one population:

	x	$(x-\bar{x})^2$	(s)	$(x-\bar{x})^2$	$(s)^2$
PH 10-1	2.81	.09	.19	.0081	.0361
PH 10-2	3.25	.53	.20	.2809	.0400
PH 10-3	2.12	.60	.09	.3600	.0081
Totals				.6490	.0842

N = 3 $\bar{x}$ = 2.73

$S_{\underline{a}}^2 = \dfrac{.649}{2} = .325$ $F = \dfrac{.325}{.028} = 11.60$

$S_{\underline{w}}^2 = \dfrac{.0842}{3} = .028$ F_{95} (2 inf.) = 2.99

An appreciation of the t test shows that the difference between the two highest samples is not significant:

	x	(s)	$(s)^2$
PH 10-1	2.81	.19	.0361
PH 10-2	3.25	.20	.0400

$\sqrt{.0361 + .0400} = .276$

3.25
− 2.81   t = .44 ÷ .276 = 1.59
  .44

A value of 1.59 standard errors would be expected to arise more than 100 times in a thousand.

A comparison of the three samples with the lowest counts again indicated the presence of more than one population:

	x	$(x-\bar{x})$	(s)	$(x-\bar{x})^2$	$(s)^2$
PH 10-3	1.55	.20	.13	.0400	.0169
PH 10-4	1.57	.18	.14	.0324	.0196
PH 10-5	2.12	.37	.09	.1369	.0081
Totals				.2093	.0446

N = 3 $\bar{x}$ = 1.75

$S_{\underline{a}}^2 = \dfrac{.2093}{2} = .105$ $F = \dfrac{.105}{.015} = 7.0$

$S_{\underline{w}}^2 = \dfrac{.0446}{3} = .015$ F_{95} (2 inf.) = 2.99

The t test again is used to compare the two lowest samples:

	x	(s)	(s)²
PH 10-3	1.55	.13	.0169
PH 10-4	1.57	.14	.0196

$\sqrt{.0169 + .0196} = .0519$

1.57
- 1.55
.02   .02 ÷ .0519 = .385

A value of .385 standard errors would arise more than 500 times in a thousand.

The grouping is therefore as follows:

TABLE II

	Counts Per Minute	Locality
PH 10-3	1.55 ± .13	Sq. 5 20-40 cm.
PH 10-4	1.57 ± .14	Sq. 2 20-40 cm.
PH 10-5	2.12 ± .09	Sq. 3 40-60 cm.
PH 10-1	2.81 ± .19	E. rear ¼ 40-60 cm.
PH 10-2	3.25 ± .20	W. rear ¼ 60-80 cm.

Thus there is a general difference in beta activity between the three levels represented and the amount of beta activity increases with the depth from which the samples were taken.

The similar activity of the two specimens from differing levels at the rear of the shelter may indicate more moist conditions in that area.

THE BETA ACTIVITY OF FOUR BONE SAMPLES FROM CUEVA RECLAU, GERONA PROVINCE, SPAIN

Charles E. Cleland
July 1962

Bone samples from Cueva Reclau (Corominas, 1946, 1949), a Spanish cave site whose occupations appear to range from Perigordian to Solutrean, were run in order to test the relationship between level of beta activity and C-14 content. The carbon-14 dates in this instance did not conform to the relative ordering of the cultural horizons from which they were derived. While the Perigordian material would have been expected to preceed the Solutrean it was instead dated at about 12,800 B.C. between the two Solutrean samples and apparently much too late. The beta activity analysis was undertaken in an attempt to clarify this discrepancy. In addition, the effects of different types of bone and different degrees of washing were also observed. The following are the amounts of beta activity for each of the samples, grouped through use of the F test.

It is possible, through the F test to place PH 12-22 in either Group I or Group II.

When the full range of data presented is considered, it appears that there is no clear agreement between the beta activity and either the C-14 dates or the reported cultural context. In all instances unwashed samples show a higher activity than washed, indicating that, in this site, soil is more active than bone. However, even after eliminating the unwashed bone and soil samples from consideration there is still no apparent order in the series with regard to either carbon-14 or cultural chronology. Our conclusion, therefore, is that ground water conditions in Cueva Reclau have not varied uniformly in horizontal and vertical loci through time.

CUEVA RECLAU

TABLE I

	Counts Per Min.	C-14 dates	Cultural Context	Bone and Preparation
Group I				
PH 12-23...	1.31 ± .06	14,800 ± 600	Perigordian	Compact and cancellous-washed
PH 12-24...	1.39 ± .14	14,750 ± 600	Perigoridan	Compact-washed
PH 12-17...	1.45 ± .12	13,200 ± 600	Solutrean	Cancellous-washed
PH 12-19...	1.49 ± .15	16,200 ± 500	Solutrean	Compact-washed
PH 12-15...	1.52 ± .10	13,200 ± 600	Solutrean	Compact-washed
PH 12-22...	1.67 ± .14	14,800 ± 600	Perigordian	Compact and cancellous-washed
Group II				
PH 12-14...	1.90 ± .14	13,200 ± 600	Solutrean	Compact-unwashed
PH 12-25...	2.00 ± .16	14,750 ± 600	Perigordian	Compact and cancellous-unwashed
PH 12-18...	2.06 ± .18	16,200 ± 500	Solutrean	Compact-washed
Group III				
PH 12-21...	3.78 ± .21	14,800 ± 600	Perigordian	Compact and cancellous-unwashed
Group IV				
PH 12-20...	4.36 ± .29	14,800 ± 600	Perigordian	Soil
PH 12-26...	4.91 ± .22	14,750 ± 600	Perigordian	Cancellous-washed
PH 12-16...	5.05 ± .27	13,200 ± 600	Solutrean	Cancellous-unwashed

A STUDY OF NATURAL RADIOACTIVITY IN OSTEOLOGICAL MATERIALS FROM THE BLACKWATER DRAW, LOCALITY NUMBER 1, ROOSEVELT COUNTY, NEW MEXICO

James E. Fitting
January 1963

The following study of beta activity in bone, dentine, and enamel is based on samples from the Blackwater Draw, Locality Number 1, Roosevelt Co., New Mexico (Sellards, 1952). Most of the materials in the study were derived from the Late Pleistocene beds in the vicinity of the Sanders Gravel Pit north of Portales, which has yielded the most complete sequence of Paleo-Indian cultural remains in western North America. The stratigraphy at the site includes the following units, from base to top: (1) basal gravel, (2) grey sand (Llano, or "Clovis" industry), (3) brown sand wedge (culture uncertain), (4) diatomite (Folsom industry), (5) Portales soil (Portales "Plano" industry), (6) jointed sand (Archaic industry).

Current estimates of age based on Carbon 14 associations found elsewhere would place the grey sand at 9000-10000 B.C. and the diatomite at about 8000 B.C. Two radiocarbon dates of about 4300 B.C. for the Portales soil horizon at Blackwater Number 1 are probably too recent.

Unless otherwise stated, samples in this study consisted of 1.5 grams of finely pulverized bone, enamel, dentine, or ivory.

Work was begun on samples from Blackwater Number 1 by Jelinek in 1958 (Jelinek and Fitting, 1963). A number of these samples were re-run in 1962 for comparative purposes. In addition to providing data on some important groupings these re-runs demonstrated to our satisfaction that the counter used in 1958 gave the same, or predictably comparable results from later equipment.

Additional material for study was sent to the Museum in 1962 by Dr. James J. Hester of the Laboratory of Anthropology, Santa Fe, New Mexico. This material consisted of thirty-two samples from Anderson Basin Number 2, Blackwater Draw Number 1, and the San Jon site. In the course of our study it was evident that a larger amount of material was needed and James

Warnica of Portales, New Mexico, sent additional material from Blackwater Draw Number 1 which he and Dr. Earl Green of the Museum, Texas Technological College, Lubbock, Texas, had collected. Several additional samples collected by Jelinek and by Hester complete the series used for this study.

For series PH 6, mostly run in the spring of 1962, a single sample was prepared from each specimen. This series was continued in the fall of 1962 with a number of runs on bison and mammoth dentine and enamel submitted by Hester. At the same time a second series, PH 14, was initiated using bison bone. For this series five separate samples were prepared from each specimen and each sample was run through the counter on two occasions. This gave us ten runs on five samples for any particular specimen and a check on the amount of internal variation of the specimen.

The PH 2 series was run in 1961 on samples of varying weights and preparation techniques. Only the 1.5 gram sample mean is used. This material was mammoth tusk from the brown sand wedge.

Certain limitations of the counting apparatus had to be taken into consideration in a study showing as great a range as the present one. The counter was designed for most effective operation on samples running up to ten counts per minute beyond background radiation. Above this level there was an increasing probability of two or more simultaneous beta emissions registering as one on the scaler. Even considering this, the maximum recording speed of the counter was about five hundred counts per minute and some of our samples approached this level. The extensive duplication of runs in the PH 14 series was an attempt to gauge the effect of chance variation on samples running over ten counts per minute.

The correction factor for voltage fluctuation was not used due to the very wide variety of activity of samples in this study.

Interpretation of Samples

Before establishing a profile it is necessary to examine the variations in radioactivity between several preparations and runs of the same sample, and the variation between samples from the same level. A number of factors have appeared to influence the count, such as species of animal, density of bone, chemical and physical condition of the bone, and the hydrological matrix.

The PH 14 series can be used to demonstrate the range of sample variation. All of these samples are from bison bone. For example, samples PH 14-1 to 5 are from a bison naviculo-cuboid from the jointed sand. Several samples were taken from different parts of a single bone as noted below.

TABLE I

Number	Run Number 1		Run Number 2	
	Count	S.E.	Count	S.E.
PH 14-1	17.39	.44	16.65	.43
PH 14-2	17.78	.42	17.95	.49
PH 14-3	18.17	.45	18.55	.38
PH 14-4	19.00	.57	17.04	.36
PH 14-5	17.41	.51	17.06	.43

This set appears quite homogeneous and needs no further comment.

Samples PH 14-6 through PH 14-10 are from a metacarpal from the jointed sand.

TABLE II

Number	Run Number 1		Run Number 2		Remarks
	Count	S.E.	Count	S.E.	
PH 14-6	28.35	.84	27.10	.80	Exterior surface
PH 14-7	25.39	.48	25.32	.67	Exterior surface
PH 14-8	38.77	.86	37.33	.99	Below exterior surface
PH 14-9	22.38	.44	22.00	.58	Exterior surface
PH 14-10	31.39	.59	29.96	.80	Below exterior surface

In this set it seems that the bone below the flaky exterior shows a higher count than the exterior surface.

Samples PH 14-11 through PH 14-15 are from a metatarsal from the jointed sand.

TABLE III

Number	Run Number 1		Run Number 2		Remarks
	Count	S.E.	Count	S.E.	
PH 14-11	16.70	.42	17.22	.48	....
PH 14-12	32.46	.46	21.59	.62	....
PH 14-13	27.83	.57	17.17	.49	....
PH 14-14	17.85	.60	17.99	.51	....
PH 14-15	11.28	.32	10.85	.27	Cancelous core

There are several aspects of this set which need examination. Both PH 14-12 and PH 14-13 appear abnormally high for the first run although the second run is within the expected range. Both samples show an abnormally high total count in relation to the uncanceled count. This is reflected in the correction factors of 1.72 for PH 14-12 and 1.35 for sample PH 14-13. While we are not using the correction factors they do indicate either (1) an unprecedented increase in cosmic radiation, or (2) irregularities in the voltage supply to the counter. The latter indication seems most likely in view of the fact that, because of construction, the power supply was cut off several times during the week they were run.

Second, PH 14-15, a sample of cancelous interior tissue, registered a lower level than the exterior samples. This is contrary to the assumption that cancelous tissue adsorbs more radioactivity than the denser exterior surface. Within our present experience this sample appears to be an exception, perhaps due to the tissue being sealed in an exterior capsule of compact bone, combined with the relatively recent stratigraphic position of the specimen.

Samples PH 14-16 through PH 14-20 are a third phalange from the carbonaceous silt.

TABLE IV

Number	Run Number 1		Run Number 2		Remarks
	Count	S.E.	Count	S.E.	
PH 14-16	11.22	.40	11.13	.36	....
PH 14-17	12.06	.32	12.34	.40	....
PH 14-18	11.82	.34	12.29	.34	....
PH 14-19	11.56	.40	10.22	.32	....
PH 14-20	13.26	.41	13.53	.36	Cancelous core

This set is quite homogeneous. It can be noted here that the cancelous core registers a higher count than the exterior samples which is in accord with most other observations on the relative activity levels of dense and cancelous bone from the same specimen.

Samples PH 14-21 through PH 14-25 are from another third phalange from the carbonaceous silt:

TABLE V

Number	Run Number 1		Run Number 2	
	Count	S.E.	Count	S.E.
PH 14-21	9.00	.34	9.36	.28
PH 14-22	9.72	.29	10.35	.30
PH 14-23	9.02	.31	9.52	.28
PH 14-24	9.02	.34	8.99	.24
PH 14-25	9.37	.30	9.04	.32

These were all exterior samples and the resulting distribution lies within a very limited range. This set can be considered to be homogeneous.

Samples PH 14-26 through PH 14-30 are from a second phalange from the carbonaceous silt:

TABLE VI

Number	Run Number 1		Run Number 2	
	Count	S.E.	Count	S.E.
PH 14-26	10.82	.34	9.89	.35
PH 14-27	11.92	.43	11.72	.30
PH 14-28	10.29	.37	11.18	.28
PH 14-29	9.81	.35	9.11	.27
PH 14-30	10.46	.36	9.33	.27

This too is a consistent set and needs no comment.

Samples PH 14-41 through PH 14-46 are from an astralagus from the diatomite.

TABLE VII

Number	Run Number 1		Run Number 2		Remarks
	Count	S.E.	Count	S.E.	
PH 14-41	105.35	1.60	106.16	1.50	Exterior ridge
PH 14-42	97.07	1.81	94.85	1.69	Exterior ridge
PH 14-43	91.52	1.76	92.94	1.45	Exterior ridge
PH 14-44	89.98	1.58	93.32	1.65	Interior
PH 14-45	97.56	1.52	....	....	Interior

There was no second run on PH 14-45. This set appears to be quite uniform.

Samples PH 14-46 through PH 14-50 are from a third phalange from the diatomite.

TABLE VIII

Number	Run Number 1		Run Number 2	
	Count	S.E.	Count	S.E.
PH 14-46	14.44	.35	13.78	.42
PH 14-47	11.23	.35	10.80	.34
PH 14-48	11.63	.33	11.54	.28
PH 14-49	10.22	.30	9.79	.31
PH 14-50	10.10	.33	9.49	.24

Although the range is somewhat greater than usual for this level of count it shows no extreme variation and is grouped for further comparative purposes.

Samples PH 14-31 through PH 14-35 are from a first phalange from the grey sand.

TABLE IX

Number	Run Number 1		Run Number 2	
	Count	S.E.	Count	S.E.
PH 14-31	333.19	4.09	365.13	4.29
PH 14-32	351.29	4.20	378.31	2.76
PH 14-33	305.69	3.92	325.13	4.11
PH 14-34	358.04	4.24	376.98	4.36
PH 14-35	386.84	4.41	433.58	4.67

This set is probably beyond the effective range of the counter and, as a result, we have a variation of over one hundred counts per minute (note that PH 14-35 is the sample with the highest count and the greatest variation). Even so, these samples can be grouped as relatively uniform in comparison to the lower level materials.

Samples PH 14-36 through PH 14-40 are from a second phalange from the grey sand.

TABLE X

Number	Run Number 1		Run Number 2	
	Count	S.E.	Count	S.E.
PH 14-36	316.19	3.99	330.03	4.08
PH 14-37	310.79	3.96	328.46	3.97
PH 14-38	328.18	4.06	351.68	4.21
PH 14-39	355.96	4.03	403.40	4.40
PH 14-40	309.69	3.95	328.28	4.07

This set exhibits the same type of range as the previous one and for the same reason it will be viewed as homogeneous for comparative purposes.

On the basis of PH 6 and PH 14 series, we will set up the interlevel and intralevel comparisons from Blackwater Draw Number 1 at the same time. For the first level, the jointed sand, we have three sets of five samples and ten runs; PH 14-1-5, PH 14-6-10, PH 14-11-15. PH 14-1-5 has a range of 16.65 to 19.00 counts per minute and was homogeneous. PH 14-6-10 showed some variation but, as we will demonstrate, this does not affect the profile. The set PH 14-11-15 shows even more variation and is admittedly skewed. Even with this irregularity it can be fitted into this grouping. All the jointed sand samples fall below 40 counts per minute. In the PH 6 series there was one dentine sample from the jointed sand, PH 6-24, registering 21.09 counts per minute.

For the carbonaceous silt we have three sets with five samples and ten runs each in the PH 14 series. These are PH 14-16-20 with a range of 10.22 to 13.53 counts per minute; PH 14-21-25 with a range of 8.99 to 10.35 counts per minute; and PH 14-26-30 with a range of 9.89 to 11.92 counts per minute. All of these samples are fairly close to each other and very homogeneous.

There are six single samples from the carbonaceous silt in the PH 6 series. Three are samples of bison long bone. They are: PH 6-25, 49.27 counts per minute; PH 6-26, 39.43 counts per minute; PH 6-52, 21.28 counts per minute. PH 6-25 appears higher than any of the PH 14 samples but it, along with the others, still falls below 50 counts per minute. There were also three samples of bison dentine which registered as follows: PH 6-37, 15.55 counts per minute; PH 6-48 (.99 grams), 98.73 counts per minute; PH 6-55 (1.5 grams), 131.13 counts per minute. These last two samples look very high—perhaps too high when it is noted that one is smaller than the other samples used.

We tested two sets from the diatomite in the PH 14 series. These were PH 14-41-45 with five samples and nine runs and a range of 89.98 to 106.16 counts per minute; and PH 14-46-50, five samples with ten runs and a range of 9.79 to 14.44 counts per minute. There are three samples of bison bone in the PH 6 series: PH 6-38, 40.41 counts per minute; PH 6-28, 82.55 counts per minute; PH 6-51, 60.12 counts per minute. There were also four samples of bison dentine from this level: PH 6-50, 452.92 counts per minute; PH 6-44, 337.15 counts per minute; PH 6-55a, 276.16 counts per minute; PH 6-56a, 362.77 counts per minute. There is a great deal of variation within the diatomite. The dentine count includes the most active specimen in the entire study while one of the PH 14 sets is close to the lowest. One of the PH 14 sets and two of the PH 6 samples fall between 50 and 150 counts per minute and the other PH 6 bone sample just borders on this range. This appears to be a well-established range for the bison bone. The set PH 14-46-50 appears to be too low, suggesting that perhaps it was intrusive.

There was a single bison long bone tested from the contact between the diatomite and grey sand. This sample, PH 6-35, runs 197.06 counts per minute which is intermediate between the counts on bone samples from the diatomite and bone samples from the grey sand.

There were no samples from the brown sand wedge in the PH 14 series but there were four bison bone samples in the PH 6 series. These were: PH 6-31, 312.93 counts per minute; PH 6-32, 410.26 counts per minute; PH 6-36, 175.06 counts per minute; PH 6-57a, 195.11 counts per minute. The first two are close enough to be grouped while the last two look most similar, in count, to the sample from the diatomite-grey sand contact sample and perhaps are from a similar contact area with the diatomite. Two other samples were tested from the brown sand wedge in the PH 6 series: PH 6-30, bison dentine, with 331.95

counts per minute; PH 6-47, mammoth ivory (.98 grams) with 217.47 counts per minute. Given equal sample weights these would probably fall in the same range. The mean of five washed 1.5 gram standard samples of mammoth tusk in series PH 2 was 244.76 c/m.

The bone samples from the grey sand were uniform and of consistently high count. There were two sets of five samples and ten runs. PH 14-31-35 varied between 305.69 and 433.58 counts per minute and PH 14-36-40 varied between 309.69 and 403.68 counts per minute. A single sample, PH 6-27, of unidentified bone, probably bison, ran 419.75 counts per minute and is consistent with the PH 14 samples. There were seven single samples of dentine and ivory as follows:

PH 6-39, bison dentine (1.05 grams), 93.17 counts per minute
PH 6-40, small horse dentine (1.01 grams), 69.17 counts per minute
PH 6-41, horse dentine (1.00 grams), 160.85 counts per minute
PH 6-42, camel dentine (.99 grams), 170.26 counts per minute
PH 6-43, peccary dentine (.99 grams), 153.18 counts per minute
PH 6-54, mammoth ivory (1.5 grams), 117.13 counts per minute
PH 6-58a, 212.85 counts per minute.

Even taking variation in species and sample size into consideration it is obvious that there is a great deal of variation in these dentine and ivory samples.

There are two samples of unidentified bone from the basal gravels. These are PH 6-45 (.98 grams), 65.75 counts per minute; PH 6-46 (1.00 gm), 66.61 counts per minute. They appear to be quite consistent and since they are our sole samples from this level they will be used in establishing a profile.

Radiometric Profile

Because of the extreme variation in ivory and dentine, the bone samples were used to establish the radiometric profile for Blackwater Draw Number 1. Dentine does absorb radioactive material quite readily but apparently at different rates. The morphology and thickness of the enamel cover, which absorbs very little radioactivity, could have an effect on this. The dentine and ivory are plotted separately on Chart II to show the variation while the bone samples and the profile are given on Chart I.

We can establish three groupings of bone values. The first of these is a low range group, under 40 counts per minute, including the jointed sands and the carbonaceous silt. The second is an intermediate range group, 50 to 150 counts per minute,

BLACKWATER DRAW, LOCALITY NUMBER 1

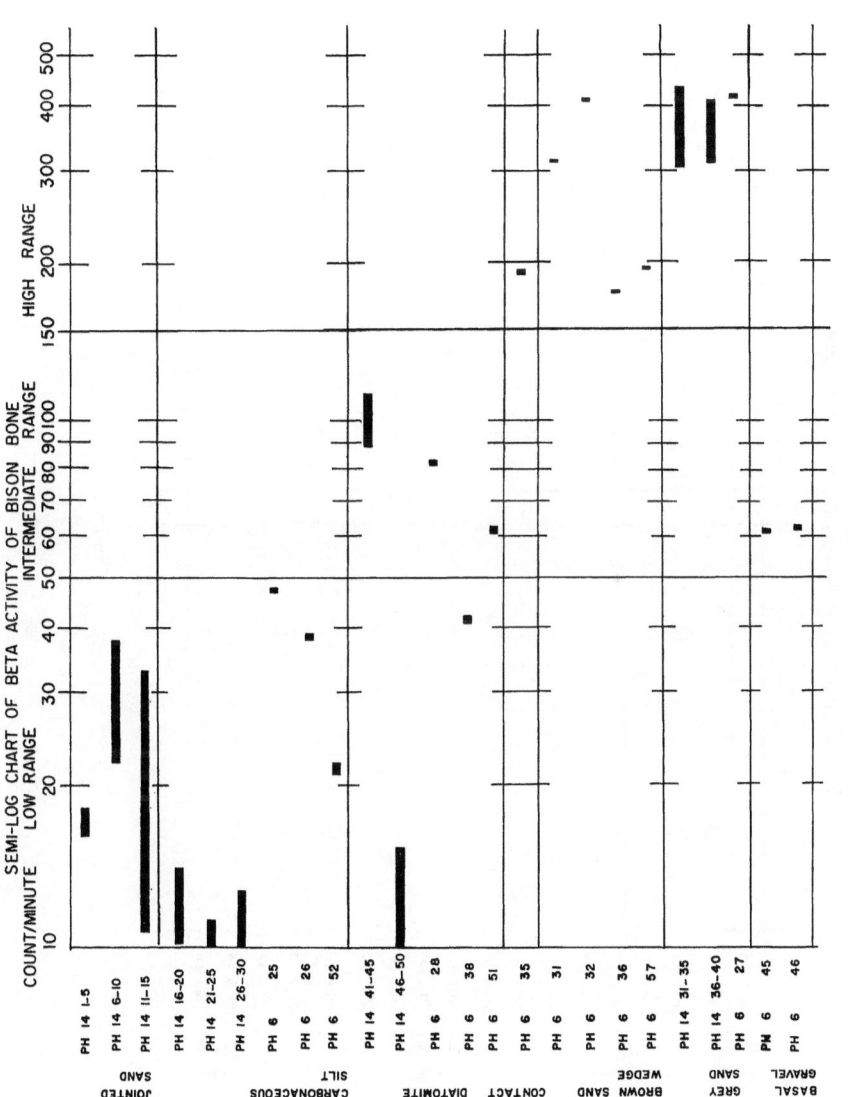

Chart I

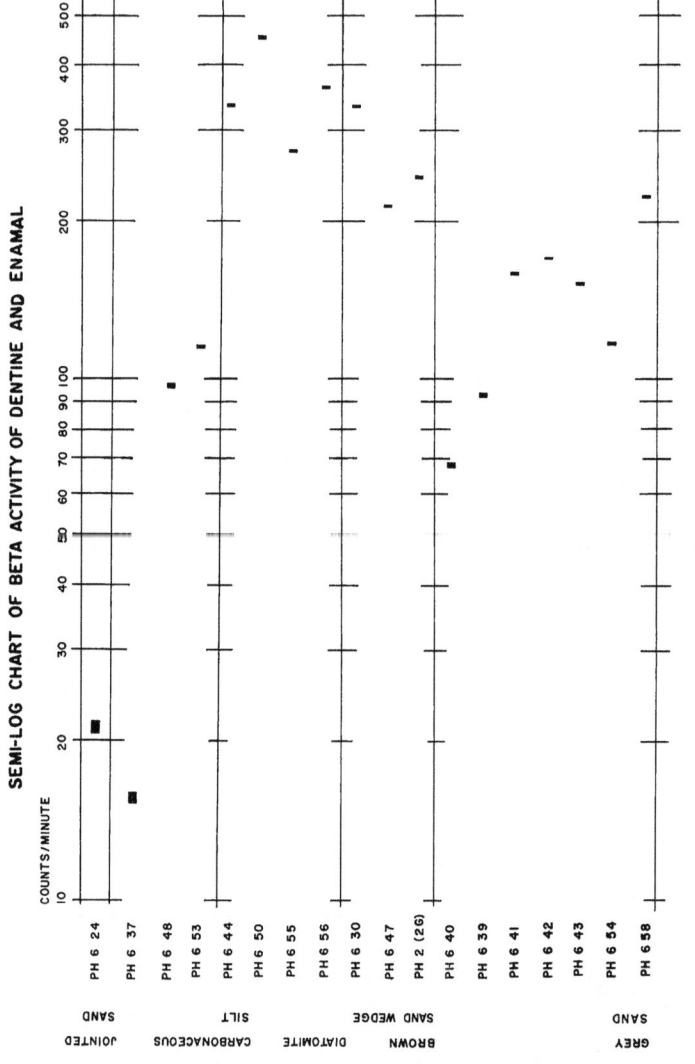

Chart II

which incorporates most of the material from the diatomite. A high range can be established including all material from brown sand wedge and grey sand. There are indications that samples from areas bordering on the diatomite may show lower counts than the samples from deeper in the deposits. All of these are higher than 150 counts per minute. While the above samples are all bison, the samples from the basal gravels are of unidentified animals. At present we do not know the full effects of species variation on accumulation of radioactive material, so it is with reservations that a drop in radioactivity to the intermediate range, 50 to 100 counts per minute, is suggested for the basal gravels.

This profile is based on radiometric examination of 29 specimens with 69 samples given a total of 120 runs through the counter. The only exceptions to the groupings outlined above are in the diatomite where two specimens fall below 50 counts per minute. The sample PH 6-38 is over 40 counts per minute and close to the intermediate range. The set PH 14-46-50 from one bison phalange falls far below this range and provides the only major exception to the profile.

The dentine and ivory samples (Chart II) were very irregular. A slight pattern can be noted, however, with an increase in radioactivity down to the diatomite, and a decline below it. This differs from the bone samples, where there is an intermediate count for the diatomite and maximum counts in the brown sand wedge and grey sand. In view of the inconsistency of samples in the upper levels, brown sand wedge and grey sand it appears difficult to establish a radiometric profile for these materials. The observed trends and consistently high counts of samples from the diatomite might serve, however, as general indicators for placement of samples.

In the fall of 1962, two additional specimens, a mammoth and bison tooth, from the brown sand wedge were submitted for comparison to see if one might be intrusive. Samples PH 6-55 through PH 6-66 were run to see if any pattern could be established. •Both enamel and dentine were run and the results are given in Table XI.

The variability of activity in dentine has been noted, indicating that the higher count of the mammoth dentine may not be significant. There is a complete overlap on the enamel count and it would therefore appear that these specimens have been subjected to the same depositional conditions.

TABLE XI

	Bison				Mammoth		
Number	Nature	Count	S.E.	Number	Nature	Count	S.E.
PH 6-57	Dentine	84.08	.92	PH 6-55	Dentine	186.23	1.60
(Run Number 2)		83.57	1.61	(Run Number 2)		186.81	2.70
PH 6-59	Dentine	115.99	1.76	PH 6-63	Dentine	131.95	2.41
PH 6-60	Dentine	111.08	2.21	PH 6-64	Dentine	166.23	3.24
PH 6-58	Enamel	21.09	.48	PH 6-56	Enamel	24.93	.52
(Run Number 2)		19.48	.62	(Run Number 2)		24.59	.43
PH 6-61	Enamel	15.29	.59	PH 6-65	Enamel	11.60	.48
PH 6-62	Enamel	16.79	.97	PH 6-66	Enamel	17.98	.64

Summary

By using the extensive bone series from Blackwater Draw Number 1 a radiometric profile has been established for this site with three major radioactivity ranges. Only two samples fell outside of the expected range for each level and only one sample is truly anamolous. The dentine and ivory samples apparently adsorb radioactive minerals differently and proved to be somewhat less predictable.

This study has served to demonstrate several things. Foremost, that consistent radiometric profiles can be established for certain areas. It has also provided information on species and bone density variation although these are not discussed in detail.

A GAMMA RAY ANALYSIS OF FOSSIL BONE FROM BLACKWATER DRAW, NUMBER 1, LOCALITY

James E. Fitting
July 1963

In July of 1963, while attempting to isolate radioactive elements in fossil bone for a proportional constituent analysis, Dr. Iqbal Qureshi recorded the gamma ray spectrum of several bone samples from Blackwater Draw. It was felt that this gamma ray analysis would be of considerable value because a major report on the beta activity of fossil bone from this locality had been prepared several months earlier.

The first report (see preceding paper) dealt with relative levels of beta activity in bone from the various geological strata at Blackwater Draw. The present study serves both as a check on the levels of activity and furnishes a qualitative assessment of the elements causing gamma radioactivity in the specimens.

Qureshi used a Phoenix Project multichannel analyzer to run one sample of uranium ore and six samples of fossil bone which I furnished. A half-hour background reading was taken and this background was subtracted from the sample readings. The samples were examined in a non-destructive manner and the results were reduced to a uniform 1 gram count whenever the sample total count was high enough to do so.

As the energy was increased gamma ray peaks were noted. Although two hundred channels were used in the analysis only the first seventy are shown in the graphs with this paper. Beyond this point differences are very minute and reach a level of significance only after extremely long runs. Sodium 22 was used to gauge the multichannel analyzer and it was found that one channel equaled N.01 (million electron volts). In the analysis of uranium ore several peaks of gamma activity were noted and are given below with the elements causing the activity:

.19 mev	uranium 235
.24 mev	radium B or lead 214
.29 mev	radium B or lead 214
.35 mev	radium B or lead 214
.61 mev	bismuth 214
.77 mev	bismuth 214
.92 mev	bismuth 214

Since only the first seventy channels are recorded on the graphs the last two bismuth peaks are not shown. A peak of .08 mev or .11 mev, or both, as well as a peak at .15 mev or .16 mev will be ignored because of the X-rays which occur at this end of the spectrum.

Figure 1 shows the spectrum of the total sample of powdered bison phalange from the jointed sand at Blackwater Draw. The uranium 235, radium B or lead 214, and bismuth 214 peaks are all present but not as prominent as the peaks in the sample of uranium ore. Qureshi suggested that any values of less than 10 counts per gram of specimen weight were unreliable. Since the total weight of the sample was 15 grams the only 1 gram value over 10 peaked at .11 mev or within the X-ray range.

Figure 2 shows the spectrum of a sample of bison phalange from the carbonaceous silt at Blackwater Draw. The curve is very similar to that of the sample from the jointed sand. The absolute level is slightly lower but like the sample from the jointed sand, all peaks fall between 20 and 100. This sample weighed 13.8 grams and when reduced to counts per gram no values over 10 were noted. In the report on beta activity of material from Blackwater Draw the samples of bison bone from the jointed sand and the carbonaceous silt were grouped into a low-level category. The sample beta counts from these strata all fell under 40 counts per minute.

Figure 3 shows the total activity of a sample of bison phalange from the diatomite at Blackwater Draw. The same peaks are present as were observed in the uranium ore but the level is lower. The level of activity of this sample is higher than that of the samples from the jointed sand and carbonaceous silt. The total count for the significant peaks falls between 100 and 300. We can chart the significant peaks for each gram of the 10.7 gram sample. This is shown in Figure 6. The significant peaks in the graph fall between 13 and 26. In the study of beta activity it was found that samples from the diatomite, for the most part, fell between 50 and 150 beta counts per minute. They were classed as intermediate range samples. This would fit well with the above gamma spectrum.

The total count of a sample of Bison Naviculo-cuboid from the brown sand wedge is shown on Figure 4. The total sample peaks fall between 100 and 800 with the exception of the .61 mev peak which is slightly below 100. The sample weighed 15.7 grams and the count per gram is given in Figure 7. The range of the peaks is between 14 and 60. The peak at .61 mev does not exceed 10 so it is not illustrated.

Figure 5 shows the total count of a sample of bison phalange from the grey sand stratum at Blackwater Draw. The total sample peaks are the highest yet observed from this area and the same is true for the count per gram peaks for this 11.1 gram sample (Figure 8). The beta activity for the brown sand wedge and the grey sand was extremely high. It formed a high level category with all values over 150 counts per minute and some over 400 counts per minute. In the report on the beta activity it was suggested that counting efficiency was lost at that high a range and that the actual beta count might be much higher. The differences between the gamma profiles of material from the brown sand wedge and the grey sand appear to bear this out.

Graphs 9 and 10 are the total sample count and the count per gram of a sample of mammoth tusk weighing 15.2 grams. This sample is from the brown sand wedge and is a part of the same standard sample used in series PH 2, Series PH 9, and in the experiments involving chemical isolation of radioactive elements in fossil bone. We have 85 runs on preparations of this standard sample and a range of between 170 and 200 beta counts per minute. This would place it within the high level beta range of material from Blackwater Draw. The gamma ray spectrum for a sample of this mammoth tusk would lead us to the same placement.

The gamma ray analysis of fossil bone and tusk from Blackwater Draw has enabled us to determine that the radioactivity of all samples was caused by uranium ore and the important decay products of uranium 235. While the absolute radio-activity of all samples was less than that of uranium ore it was possible to pick out three distinct groupings. The samples from the jointed sand and carbonaceous silt (Figs. 1 and 2) were very low, the samples from the diatomite occupied an intermediate position (Figs. 3 and 6) and samples from the brown sand wedge and grey sand all showed a relatively high level of activity. This is in perfect agreement with the grouping developed in the study of beta activity. It has also been shown that the same radioactive materials are present in both bison bone samples and the sample of mammoth tusk.

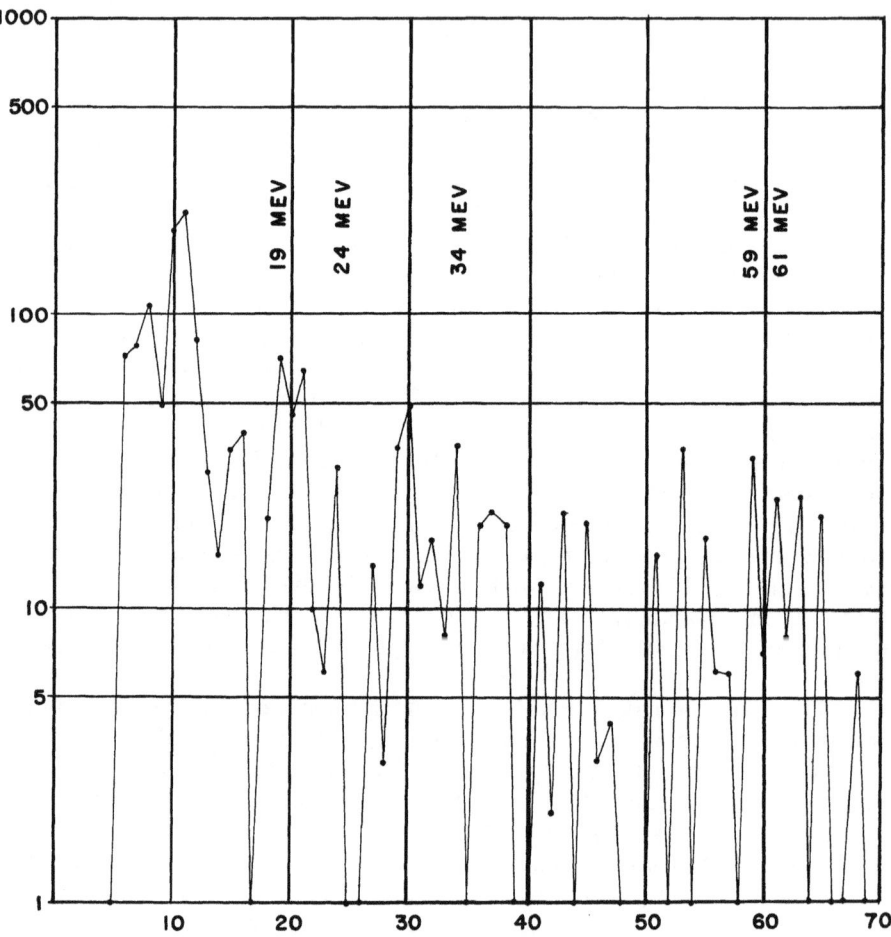

Fig. 1. Total radioactivity of a sample of bison bone from the jointed sand level.

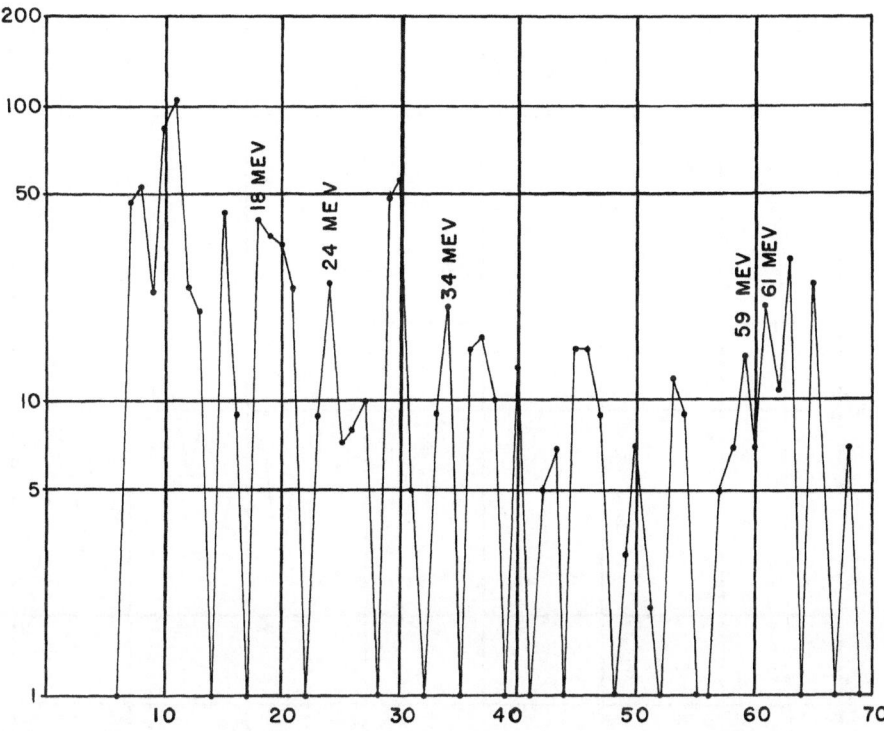

Fig. 2. Total radioactivity of a sample of bison bone from the carbonaceous silt level.

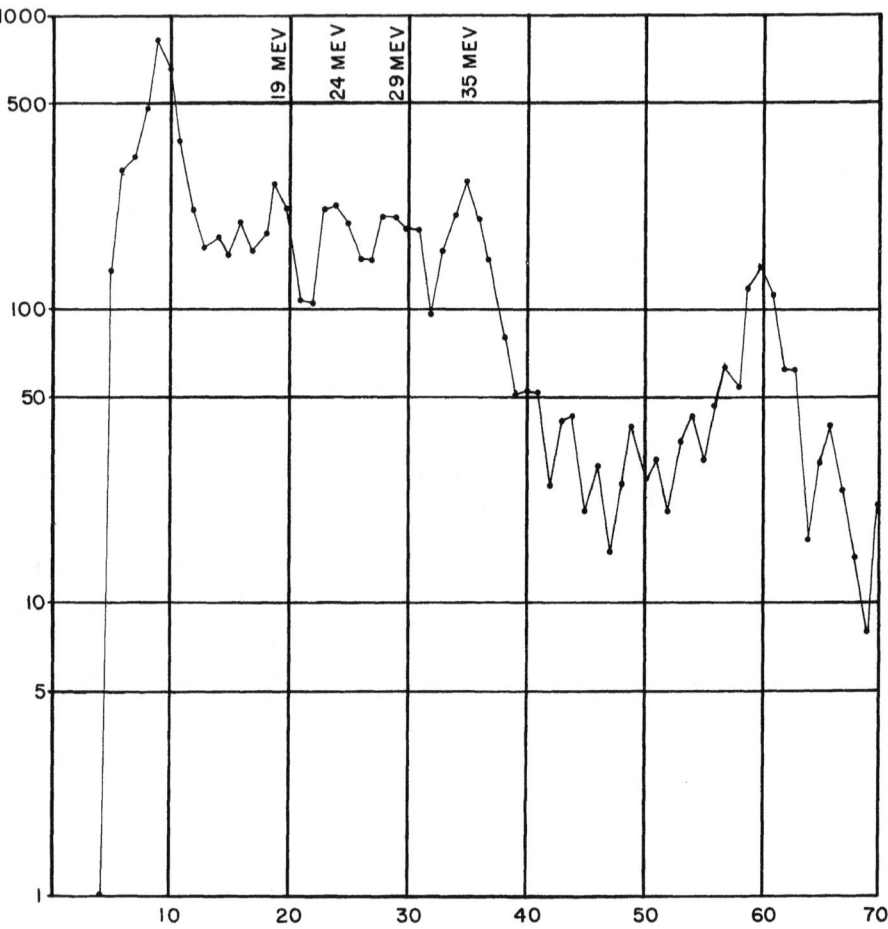

Fig. 3. Total radioactivity of a sample of bison bone from the diatomite level.

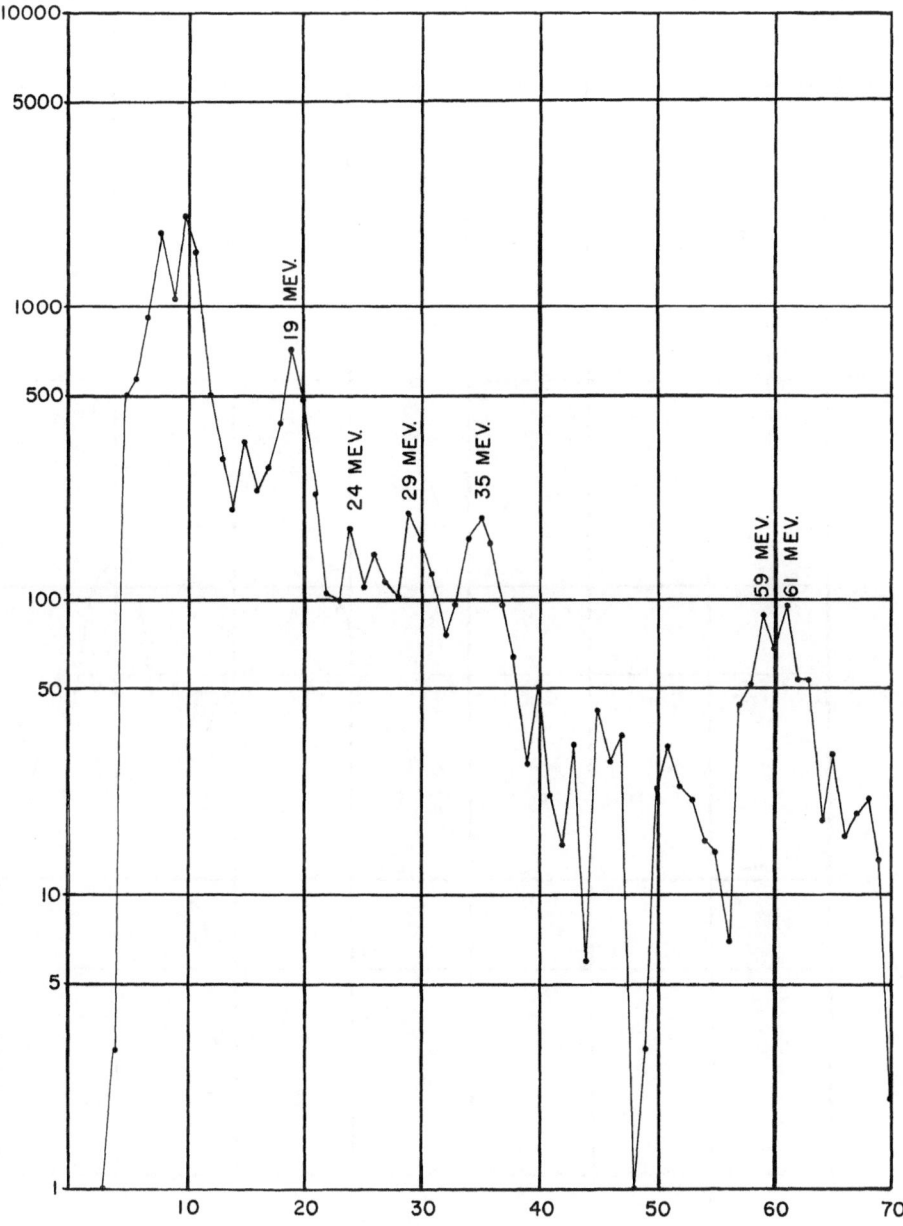

Fig. 4. Total radioactivity of a sample of bison bone from the brown sand wedge.

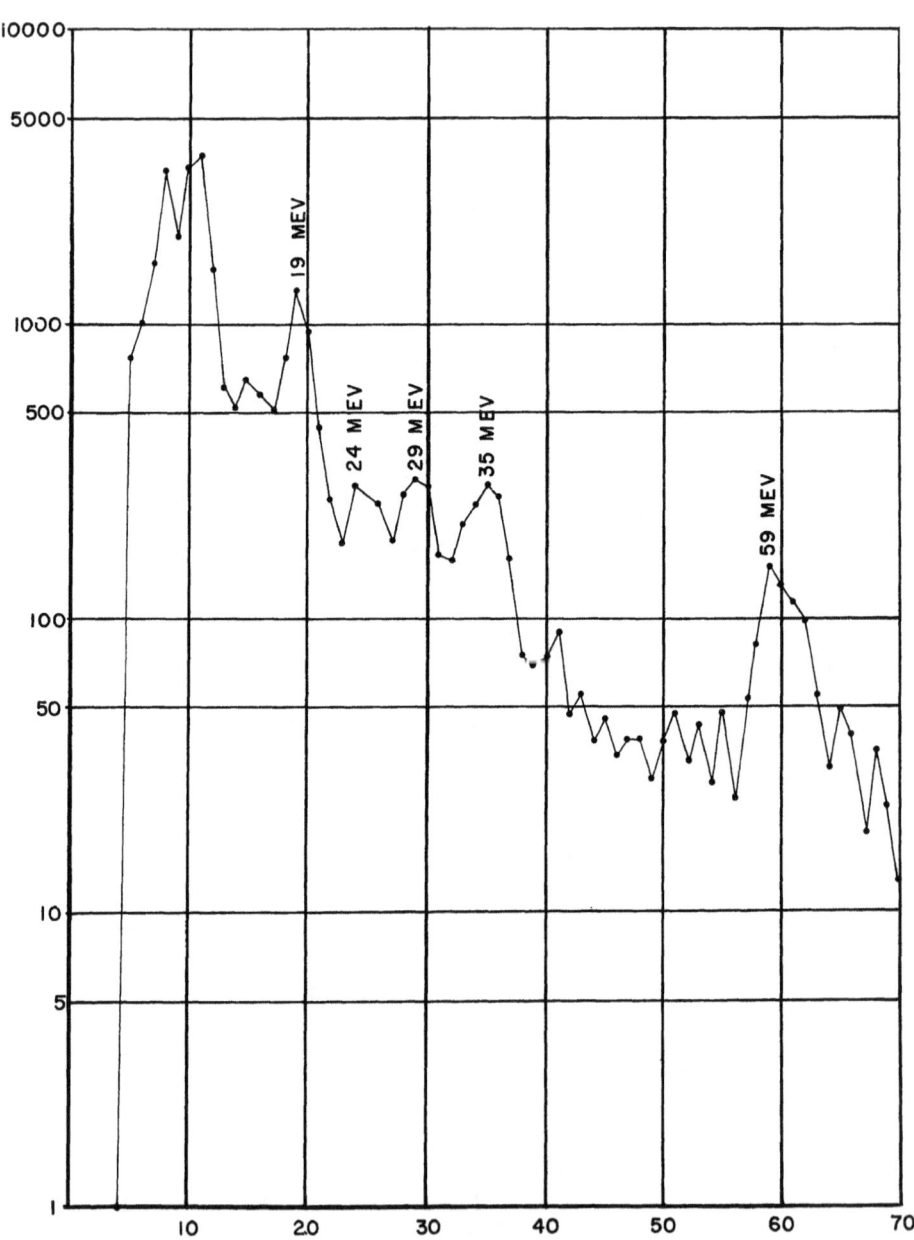

Fig. 5. Total radioactivity of a sample of bison bone from the grey sand level.

BLACKWATER DRAW: GAMMA ANALYSIS

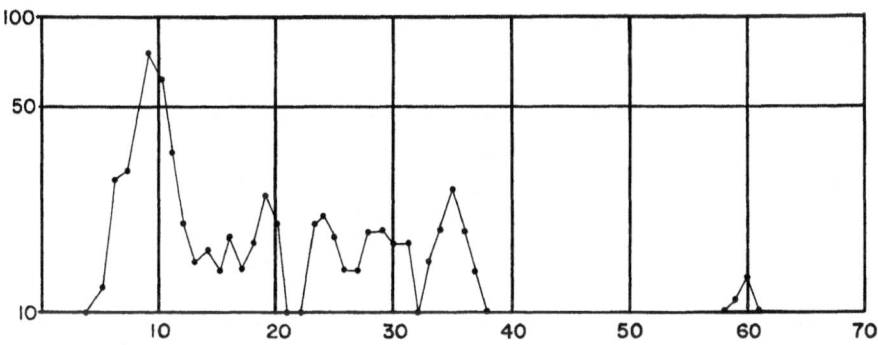

Fig. 6. Radioactivity per gram of a sample of bison bone from the diatomite level.

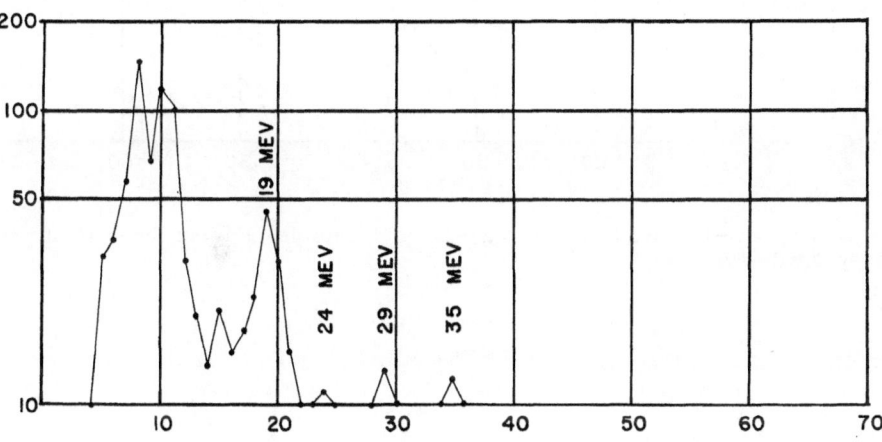

Fig. 7. Radioactivity per gram of a sample of bison bone from the brown sand wedge.

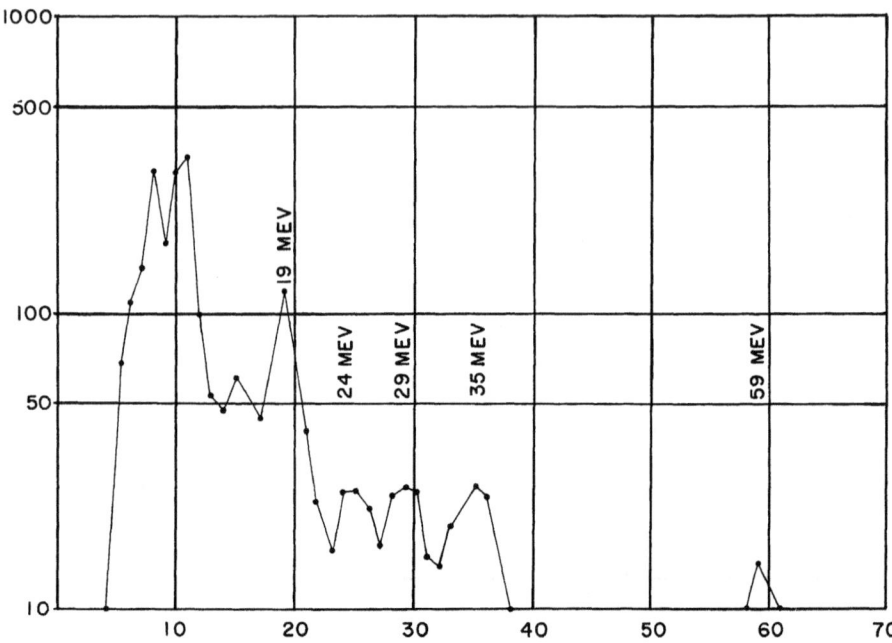

Fig. 8. Radioactivity per gram of a sample of bison bone from the grey sand level.

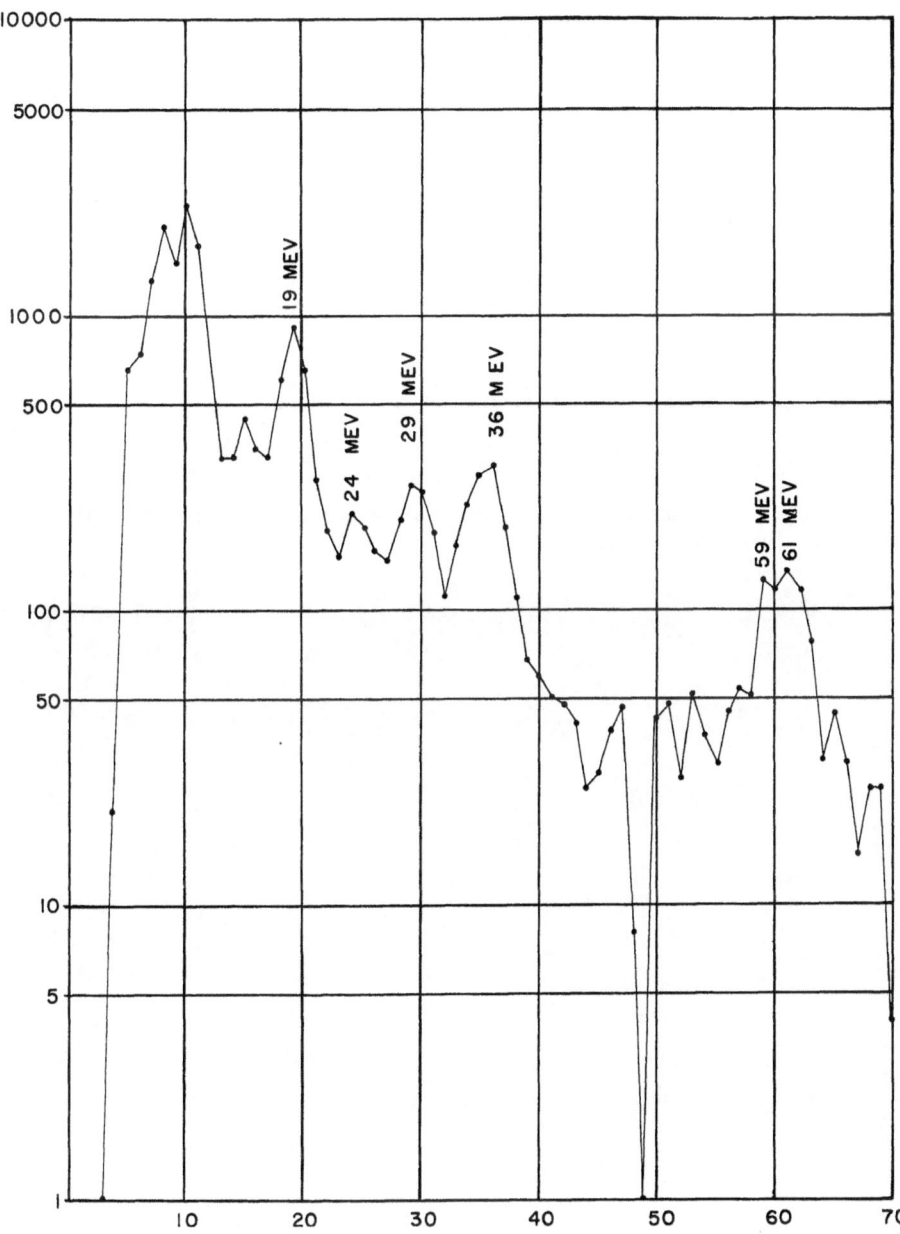

Fig. 9. Total radioactivity of a sample of mammoth tusk from the brown sand wedge.

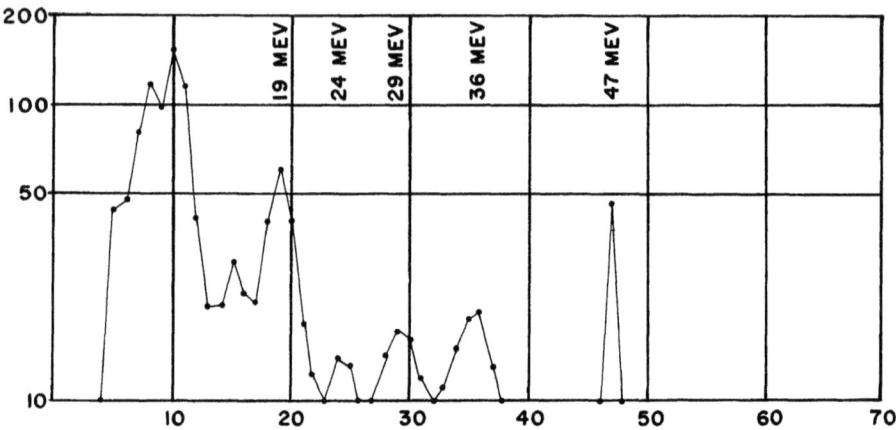

Fig. 10. Radioactivity per gram of a sample of mammoth tusk from the brown sand wedge.

ADDENDUM

CHEMICAL ISOLATION OF RADIOACTIVE ELEMENTS IN ARCHAEOLOGICAL AND PALEONTOLOGICAL MATERIAL

James E. Fitting
July 1963

The purpose of this study was to attempt to provide an easy method for the gross identification of radioactive substances causing beta activity in fossil bone. The main problem we faced was that of finding a method which could be used by an archaeologist working in a modest museum laboratory, rather than by a chemist.

In June and July of 1963 Dr. Iqbal Qureshi of the Pakistan Atomic Energy Commission, while teaching at the University of Michigan, worked with me on a simplified process for isolating radioactive elements in archaeological and paleontological material. The methods presented in this paper were suggested by Qureshi. I acted, for the most part, as an observer and recorder.

The material selected for the experiment was part of a standard sample of mammoth tusk from Blackwater Draw. This standard sample had been used for a number of tests from 1961 to 1963.

In 1961, ten 1-gram samples from this specimen had ranged between 179.79 counts per minute and 200.65 counts per minute with a mean of 191.94 counts per minute. The 1962 series was a test for internal variation of a standard sample. There were 5 separate runs on 15 preparations of the standard sample. They ranged between 171.85 counts per minute and 194.14 counts per minute with a mean of 184.68 counts per minute. The mean of all 85 runs on 1-gram preparations from this standard sample was 186.53 counts per minute. This gave us an idea of what the total activity of sample fractions should be after analysis. In 1963 a qualitative analysis of the specimen was made, using a multichannel analyzer.

The first step in our procedure was to carefully weigh out 1 gram of standard sample using an analytical balance. The gram of standard sample was dissolved in nitric acid. Six mole strength HNO_3 is most effective although concentrated nitric acid with a small amount of water added would serve the purpose. The solution was heated over a hot plate and brought to a boil. The nitric acid was allowed to boil away and the residue was again dissolved using nitric acid or water. It was emphasized that as little liquid as possible should be used for dissolving the material the second time (gentle heat helps to dissolve the residue in the second solution more quickly).

After the second dissolution there was a small amount of insoluble residue in the beaker. The solution was filtered and this residue was collected and saved on a filter paper. The beaker was rinsed with distilled water which was also passed through the filter. Rubber gloves should be worn while handling the acid solution during the filtering process. The filter paper was later counted in a low-level beta counter and showed the beta activity in this part of the sample was caused by thorium and other insoluble decay products.

The next step was to isolate radium, an important uranium decay product and the suspected cause of much of the radioactivity in the sample. This was done by precipitating barium sulfate and radium sulfate. In our initial experiment we added 20 ml of barium carrier to enrich the barium of the sample. This was found to be too much as too large a quantity of precipitate was formed. Some of our count was, no doubt, lost because of self-absorption during the counting process. It is suggested that in future experiments, no barium carrier be used. If, in low-level material, it is necessary to add barium carrier extremely small amounts should be used at first. The carrier is made by dissolving barium chloride in distilled water.

Barium sulfate was precipitated by adding a 5 per cent solution ammonium sulfate $(NH_4)_2SO_4$, and warming the solution until the precipitate formed. There is a tendency for the material in the beaker to "spit" over direct heat, and an indirect heating technique is suggested for future work. In our initial experiments a centrifuge was used to accelerate the precipitation process. This was necessary because of the large amount of barium carrier which we added and the correspondingly large quality of barium sulfate.

The precipitate was recovered in filter paper. The supernatant was collected in a filter flask with the use of a water flow to evacuate the air from the flask and speed the recovery of the precipitate.

Qureshi suggested that the samples be covered with Saran Wrap until they are counted. He had found that Scotch Tape and other covers absorbed radiation.

ADDENDUM

We attempted to evaporate the supernatant on a hot plate but the tendency to "spit" was even greater here than in the previous instance. An alternative method of evaporation was tried. The supernatant was poured into a planchet and evaporated under an infrared light. This took approximately one hour but the process could have been speeded up by using a larger planchet.

The supernatant count reflected the uranium content. Other elements with beta radiation might have been present but it is logical to assume that uranium, because of its long half-life, is the primary cause of beta radiation in this part of the sample.

Due to technical difficulties the counter designed by Professor Crane was unavailable for these samples and they were processed in a suitable counter at the University of Michigan School of Public Health through the courtesy of Mr. Charles Pelletier.

At this point we had three samples; a residue from the first dissolution, a barium precipitate, and a supernatant. The resultant levels of beta activity are given below:

Residue . . . . 6.37 counts per minute
Precipitate . . . . 89.40 counts per minute
Supernatant . . . . 78.40 counts per minute
Total . . . . .174.17 counts per minute

It can be seen that the resultant total falls within the range of single samples of the standard samples. This is probably fortuitous, for small amounts of the sample were lost in processing and beta activity was absorbed by the excess barium sulfate. These losses were compensated for by the increased counted efficiency for lower level samples. As a result, the total count appears to fall within the range of 1-gram sample counts.

From the results it can be seen that very little of the beta activity is caused by insoluble radioactive elements. The residue count was only 6.37 counts per minute and accounts for 3.7 per cent of the total sample activity. The precipitate and the supernatant have a higher level of radioactivity and are very similar. The precipitate shows a higher count and, with the beta absorption in the heavy precipitate the actual count may be even higher. Radium in the precipitate accounts for 51.3 per cent of radioactivity of the sample. The possible Uranium count does not exceed 45 per cent of the sample count. This suggests that Oakley and Rixon's (1958) assumption that the radioactivity of samples from the Scharbauer site was caused by a radioactive isotope of Uranium was an oversimplification. It would be logical to expect the occurrence of a large number of decay products and the isolation of Radium D demonstrates this. Investigation with the multichannel analyses demonstrated that the radioactivity of fossil bone from Blackwater Draw was caused by the entire decay spectrum of uranium ore, and this is essentially the result obtained from the quantitive assay which we have just described.

SUMMARY

Arthur J. Jelinek

The preceding reports offer several contributions to our knowledge of the relationships between the natural radioactivity of prehistoric materials and relative chronology. The relationships that are found, within the limits of present research techniques, are of an order that is easily obscured by several intervening variables.

The present research efforts, therefore, have been largely concerned with the development of the fundamental techniques of sample selection and preparation that provide for the maxiumum comparability of results. It is to be hoped that the resolution of these basic problems will clear the way for more extensive research.

In the development of techniques of sample preparation, it has become clear that the cleaning of bone specimens is of considerable importance because of the differences of activity of soils and bone. In bone samples of low activity, adhering soil will raise the apparent level of activity (Cueva Reclau, p. 62), while in high activity samples the adhering impurities will dilute the activity of a sample (Effect of Sample Preparation, p. 8). It would appear that very small soil particles can be responsible for much of the activity (Effect of Particle Size, p. 14). It is also clear that the weight and activity of a sample are directly related and that standard weights of samples are essential for accurate comparison (Effect of Sample Preparation).

In comparing the samples of bone from any single deposit, several key variables can be isolated. While there is some suggestion of variability of bone across species in ability to adsorb radioactive minerals (Riverside Cemetery, p. 28), it appears more likely that most variation of this sort is due to textural and size differences in bones, as is most strikingly demonstrated in differences between cancellous and compact bone from similar contexts (Lloyd's Rock Hole, p. 32; PH 12-24, PH 12-26 from Cueva Reclau, p. 62). The relatively high activity of cancellous bone in these instances may perhaps be ascribed to the greater surface area of this type of bone relative to volume. It is important to note, however, that these relationships do not invariably hold true (PH 12-17 and PH 12-15 from Cueva Reclau p. 62; PH 14-15 from Blackwater Draw Number 1, p. 64). It is quite possible that (as Cleland points out with respect to fish vertebrae, p. 58) the difficulties of cleaning relatively porous bone may lead to more distortion of count in cancellous tissue due to remnant soil particles. Therefore, markedly higher beta counts from cancellous bone in samples of generally low activity and markedly lower counts in this type of bone from high activity samples should be investigated further. An additional variable discovered in the studies of bone concerns the variation in activity of compact tissue at and below the surface of the specimen (PH 14-6 to 10, Blackwater Draw Number 1, p. 66). Again, this may be largely a textural difference since the surface of the bone specimen mentioned appeared somewhat more friable than the interior. Within the limits of our studies it does not appear that any of the varieties of heat-alteration of bone likely to be encountered by the prehistorian affects the natural radioactivity. There are promising indications that most of the textural variables could be overcome if the bone material for any single profile were restricted to comparable tissue and treated chemically as a solution and precipitate, to achieve uniform density and avoid distortion due to backscattering (Jelinek and Fitting, 1963: 534-35).

The indication that natural radioactivity in bone exhibiting a high level of activity is due not only to uranium, but also to the presence of decay products of uranium in significant amounts leads us to conclude that counts interpreted as parts per million of uranium oxide do not always express accurately the relationships between the samples. This finding confirms Oakley's (1963: 30) hypothesis regarding the presence of "daughter elements."
If it is possible to assume that the material initially deposited in the bone consisted entirely of a uranium compound, then it would seem that there exists a very promising method of determining absolute chronology on the basis of ratio of decay products to uranium in radioactive bone. This method would not be restricted by the wide variation in activity between localities, as is relative dating based on gross activity.

In samples of bone exhibiting a very low level of activity, the untested possibility continues to exist that this activity may be due to elements other than uranium. The anomalous activity of samples from the Riverside Cemetery (p. 28) suggests the possibility that some Carbon-14 is being counted, leading to an impression of lower activity with age. It is also clear that the activity of soils may be due to a wide variety of materials, including soluble compounds derived from recent fallout.

SUMMARY

In conclusion, it has been shown that the natural radioactivity of prehistoric materials, particularly bone, can be widely utilized in problems of relative chronology; however, the interpretations of this radioactivity must consider a wide range of variables subjected to careful methodological control.

REFERENCES

Binford, Lewis, R.
    1960   Analysis of the Radioactive Properties of Bone Specimens from the Smith Site, Delaware County, Oklahoma. Museum of Anthropology, University of Michigan (ditto copy). Ann Arbor.
    1962   Radiometric Analysis of Bone Material from the Oconto Site. The Wisconsin Archeologist, Vol. 43, No. 2, pp. 31-41. Lake Mills.

Bowie, S. H. U., and C. F. Davidson
    1955   The Radioactivity of the Piltdown Fossils. Bulletin of the British Museum (Natural History), Geology, Vol. 2, No. 6, pp. 276-82. London.

Braidwood, Robert J., and Bruce Howe
    1960   Prehistoric Investigations in Iraqui Kurdistan. Studies in Ancient Oriental Civilization No. 31. Chicago.

Corominas, J. M.
    1946   La Cueva del Reclau-Viuer de Serina. Anales del Instituto de Estudios Gerundensis, V. 1, p. 209. Gerona.
    1949   El paleolitico superior en la Cueva Reclau-Viuer de Serina (Espana). Rivista di Scienze Preistoriche, Vol. IV, pp. 44-54. Rome.

Crane, H. R., and James B. Griffin
    1960   University of Michigan Radiocarbon Dates V. American Journal of Science, Radiocarbon Supplement, Vol. 2. New Haven, Conn.

Davidson, Charles F., and D. Atkin
    1953   On the Occurrence of Uranium in Phosphate Rock. Compte Rondu, XIXe Congrès Géological International, Vol. XI, No. 11, 13-31. Paris.

Guilday, John E.
    1964   New Paris No. 4: A Pleistocene Cave Deposit in Bedford County, Pennsylvania. Bulletin of the National Speleological Society, Vol. 26, No. 4. Arlington, Va.

Herbert, C.
    1947   Contribution a l'étude de la chimie des phosphates de calcium. Annals des Mines, Vol. 136, mem. 4. Paris.

Hill, W. S.
    1950   Elementes radioactivos en los nuesos fósiles del Tercianio y del cuantennario. Ciencia e investigacion, Vol. 2, p. 1. Monte Video.

REFERENCES

Jaffee, Elizabeth B., and A. M. Sherwood
    1951   Physical and Chemical Comparison of Modern and Fossil Tooth and Bone Material. V.S.G.S. TEM-149. Oak Ridge, Tenn.

Jelinek, Arthur J.
    1960a   A Late Pleistocene Vertebrae Fauna from Texas. Journal of Paleontology, Vol. 34, No. 5, pp. 933-39. Bridgewater.
    1960b   An Archaeological Survey of the Middle Pecos River Valley and the Adjacent Llano Estacado. Doctoral Dissertation, University of Michigan, Ann Arbor.

Jelinek, Arthur J., and James E. Fitting
    1963   Some Studies of Natural Radioactivity in Archaeological and Paleontological Materials. Papers of the Michigan Academy of Science, Arts, and Letters, Vol. 48 (1962 meeting), pp. 531-40. Ann Arbor.

Neuman, W. F., M. W. Neuman, Edna R. Main, and B. J. Mulryan
    1949   The Deposition of Uranium in Bone (Parts IV-VI). The Journal of Biological Chemistry, Vol. 179, No. 1, pp. 325-48. Baltimore.

Oakley, Kenneth P.
    1950   Relative Dating of the Piltdown Skull. The Advancement of Science, Vol. 6, No. 24, pp. 343-44. London.
    1955   Analytical Methods of Dating Bones. Ibid., Vol. 12, No. 45, pp. 3-8. London.
    1963   Analytical Methods of Dating Bones. In D. Brothwell and E. Higgs, Science and Archaeology. London.

Oakley, Kenneth P., and Arthur E. Rixon
    1958   The Radioactivity of Materials from the Scharbauer Site, Near Midland, Texas. American Antiquity, Vol. 24, No. 2, pp. 185-87. Salt Lake City.

Sellards, E. H.
    1952   Early Man in America. University of Texas Press. Austin.

Spaulding, Albert C.
    1958   The Significance of Differences Between Radiocarbon Dates. American Antiquity. Vol. 23, No. 3, pp. 309-11. Salt Lake City.

Strutt, R. J.
    1908   The Accumulation of Helium in Geological Time. Proceedings of the Royal Society of London, Series A, Vol. 81, p. 277. London.

www.ingramcontent.com/pod-product-compliance
Lightning Source LLC
Jackson TN
JSHW070313120426
100741JS00007B/50